The Successful Ministry of Community Service Chaplaincy

By Jake Popejoy

"Successfully pastoring a community in our present age."

Table of Contents

Introduction

Community Service has long been a mantra for politicians, sociologists, community organizers, as well as many Pastors and church leaders. Many of us, as pastors, would totally agree with the process and activities of Community Service as a strategic concept for the betterment and growth of our church, community and nation. If we show our face in the community, then the community can see the face of the church, and hopefully some aspect of our God and Saviour.

The intent of this book is to highlight Community Service as a ministry and outreach. We can do this through a ministry of Chaplaincy. Thus, Community Service Chaplaincy as the medium or tool for reaching, helping and ministering to our communities. Accordingly, we ask, what is Community Service Chaplaincy? Chaplains, unlike pastors or ministers are focused on the hurting and needs of people regardless of any specific denominational or organizational affiliation. Chaplains are caregivers of the premier order.

Of course the question, indicated above, can only be answered from the perspective of the person asking the question. What does the person asking the question mean by the term Community Service? In, and of itself, community service can be seen as a form of discipline for lawbreakers, such as picking up trash along the highway, menial tasks, or volunteer service. Community service can also be performed to work off a debt or a correctional sentence. Additionally, Community service can be the getting a "merit badge" as a Boy Scout or Girl Scout does, or can be part of the requirements to be part of a youth group, etc.

With regard to the Church or para-church organizations, Community Service Chaplaincy better enables these organizations to care for people "beyond the gates" of the local church. It is an avenue to help those who are hurting, lonely, in crisis or destitute. Community Service Chaplains require a purposeful, but not necessarily a lengthy and extensive training regiment. However, the training must provide an understanding of key issues, concepts and skills necessary to facilitate effective community ministry and empower the local church pastor and lay leadership to genuinely care for others by reaching out to hurting humanity in the church and local community. This ministry becomes a network of Community Service Chaplains who are dedicated to taking care, benevolence and ministry outside the walls of the traditional church to agencies both public and private.

Why Community Service Chaplaincy? The historical role of the pastor remains vital to the nurturing and growth of the church with regard to heritage, theology and vision. Yet the church does not appear to be transitioning quickly enough in order to present the gospel message into a secular and pluralistic society. The fundamental goal of the Church is to continue with care and evangelism, which must, emphatically, be present in order to deliver God's message to this complex generation that we serve.

Timothy L. Lull, in his article "Reshaping the Mission of the Church", states, "For the church to have a future there must be a mission ... more than passing on the faith to one's biological children."[1] It is clearly the opinion

---

[1] Timothy F. Lull, "Reshaping the Mission of the CHURCH," *USA*

of the author that Community Service Chaplaincy is that needed mission. In order to advance Community Service and ultimately be an asset to our church and community the Community Service Chaplain must be able to identify five trends, which are shaping the churches and congregations of the 21st. These trends are impacting the churches of North America, Western Europe and to a certain degree South America. By identifying these trends, the church will be better equipped to present Chaplaincy and ministry to a waiting community.

- <u>First, the passing of Christendom.</u> In more and more places in North America and Western Europe, active church-going Christians will live

Today (Society for the Advancement of Education), July 2000, 58 [database on-line]; available from Questia, http://www.questia.com/; Internet; accessed 10 July 2005.

as a minority of the population in the 21st century. This trend is nothing new, being long developed in Europe--first in its Protestant north, and then, since Vatican II, in many traditional Roman Catholic countries as well. Countries such as France, Belgium, Sweden and Holland, to name a few, are quickly secularizing. While the change is coming quite unevenly in various parts of North America, it does so with a special sense or perception of threatening to many who hold faith in the Christian doctrines.

Many church members feel that they remember better days for the church, with larger crowds, more influence, and fewer financial problems. We live increasingly around and among those who feel little or no pressure toward religious affiliation, and many of the children of religious parents are not churched in any active way. We, the church, must now seek, more than ever for opportunities of ministry, which may possibly defy, and to a degree, conflict with the paradigms of traditional ministry models.

Nevertheless, wherever Christendom has thrived, until recently, there tends to be deep discouragement at its passing. It takes a great shift in attitude to avoid depression and discouragement, and a genuine theological vision to see opportunity, rather than decline. In these changes, Christians are being forced to question if they are to have a religious or church future at all. Canadian theologian Douglas J. Hall states, "Until we become courageous enough to go with our contemporaries (and especially the most victimized of our contemporaries) into the dark night of the eclipse of meaning, we shall not have a gospel that speaks to the real situation of our time and place."[2] In other words, if we are not prepared to go into places that the church has previously been criticized and if we do not develop a ministry model which includes those who, presently, have no interest in the traditional church then our future as an influencing factor

---

[2] Douglas John Hall, "Confessing Christ in a Post-Christendom Context," *The Ecumenical Review* 52, no. 3 (2000): 410 [database on-line]; available from Questia, http://www.questia.com/; Internet; accessed 11 July 2005.

on this earth is certainly, at best, bleak. In order to do this, however, we must, influence and "win" the pastor to a new model, before we are allowed to convince the church at large.

The absolute and imperative of ministry is to have, and maintain identification with the needy and victimized of our society in order to have a ministry of care, which reaches the lost. Douglas Hall may be idealistic in his presentation, yet the message is clear. Evangelism, when preceded by caregiving will have a divine impact on our society.

- <u>Second, the unchurched as formerly churched</u>. The task of trend identification is greatly complicated by the fact that so many of the people who are outside the church were at one time church members. It is a great challenge to take the Christian story to those who have never heard it, but a double challenge to convince those with earlier and negative experience of the Christian community to give the church another try. This is actually a great obstacle, for most Christians know of someone who has been hurt, humiliated or rejected by the church. Consequently, to encourage these back into the fold, will take a different type of ministry. It will take a Chaplaincy rather than a traditional pastoral process.

In spite of the spiritual scar tissue among former church members, many of the aforementioned, will ardently, still consider themselves Christians. Therefore, simple appeals to church visits and traditional attempts at evangelism are inadequate. Even the warmest and most-welcoming church will not easily receive a visit from those whose memories of the church are of law, judgment, or even boredom. Compound this with the thinking of Ron McManus, who asks the question if we are a church, which is friendly, or are we a church that makes friends? His point being, that most unchurched people don't necessarily look for a friendly church, but rather they come to church in search of a friend. One of the uniqueness's of chaplaincy is the ability to establish relationships and friendships that do not require, in any way, a theological posit in order to do so.

We must of course realize that one does not have to take all of the complaints of the formerly churched at face value, for at times they may give an unfair representation of the churches which they describe, yet, the impression that religion is a source of strife, judgment, exclusion, or obscure and unhelpful dogma is a challenge that few local communities have really pondered. Do we, the ministers and servants of the church ever see anything in parish life and public witness, which challenges the perception of the church as a negative institution? If we are so myopic as to see that the church has shot itself in the foot from time to time, we will have little hope of making necessary corrections for the future generations of the church.

- <u>Third, residential religious pluralism.</u> Church congregations live surrounded by neighbors who practice many forms of Christianity, as well as by those who have no formal religious affiliation at all. A new factor in recent decades is the presence of adherents of the major world religions in many local communities--especially metropolitan centers. The traditional definition of World Missions has changed, whether we like it or not. Some of our traditional denominations do not like it and cannot easily abide it. Why? To change the present definition of World Missions would be to radically change the internal political and financial structures of many denominations. Office holders would be challenged, budgets would be challenged and certain perks, such as world travel would be questioned.

While many worthwhile missionaries and projects are funded by the generosity of local churches and individual donors, it will become incumbent upon the church to develop a form of volunteer missionaries. These missionaries may no longer leave native soil to take the gospel to foreign lands, but rather will find their mission field in the complexity of community agencies, industrial plants and a wide array of societal groups and sub-cultures.

- <u>Fourth, the shaping of churches and congregations must be seen with objective evangelical and caring eyes.</u> Thus identifying that the Christian churches' world mission is now a local mission in the cities, and even to some extent, in smaller towns, as one's neighbors and co-workers may be Muslim, Buddhist, Hindu, or adherents of other traditional non-Christian religions. A number of Christians have not really got past the bigotry toward Jews. But now, the Jews may appear to be closer or more familiar neighbors as the Christian Church encounters more-distant individuals (regarding faith groups) many of whom are not likely to join their churches or as they consider Christianity with a hostile view.

Religious pluralism is really nothing new, but the history of Christianity in the way that this pluralism is dealt with must change. There was a time that religious pluralism was dealt with from a perspective of condescending dialogue to such harshness as the intolerance of the crusades and inquisitions. Not any more, political and social values will not permit such a thing and it is clear that the Gospel requires another Way.

The new factor for many Christians is the closeness and immediacy of these other options, creating a familiarity of residential pluralism. As people become friends and co-workers, children attend school together, and intermarriage looms as a real possibility, the secure sense of living as a Christian in a Christian culture is deeply challenged. More signs of conflict are seen at this point in the church's history than evidence of local congregations dealing positively with how to live together in this new situation. It is important for the Community Service Chaplain to remember, that our mission is not to simply get people to "live together", but rather to develop a ministry model whereby we can establish relationships for the ultimate purpose of confirming the Gospel in the hearts of all men. Again, Timothy Lull states, *"The minimal first step would be opportunities to learn more about the religions of these neighbors, but few congregations have an effective parish education structure for adults that could take up this teaching challenge."*[3]

- <u>Finally, The ambiguity of new technologies.</u> Finally, the other striking trend that is influencing all aspects of life, including the religious, is the pervasive presence of new technologies. It has not become completely clear what the influence may be from the presence of computers, the Internet, social media, and all the other means that make local communities less isolated than in the past. In one way, these

---

[3] Timothy F. Lull, "Reshaping the Mission of the CHURCH," *USA Today (Society for the Advancement of Education)*, July 2000, 58 [database on-line]; available from Questia, http://www.questia.com/; Internet; accessed 10 July 2005.

diverting opportunities may drive us all into a personal form of sectarianism, or at least into pervasive isolation with "virtual" opportunities of social media, such as personal , web streaming and dedicated websites. In another respect, these technologies offer a great possibility for the reconnection of the church, with support and resources becoming available to a local congregation.

There may be deeply negative aspects of this new technology, especially if the continuing explosion of technological possibilities drives a fresh wedge between the rich and the poor and the young and the older. For example, we must recognize that online ministry, obviously only reaches those with the financial and technical acumen to "go online". Although this is rapidly changing in South America, his presently leaves much of the underdeveloped nations without adequate means to receive this form of ministry. Add to this, there is no practical way for "online ministries" to meet physical and benevolent needs presently. The Community Service Chaplain has the mandate to care before evangelizing. Hence, caring will more often than not, require a physical presence. Chaplains are trained, prepared and exceptionally good at the "ministry of presence".

However, there are also reasons to be hopeful that this set of new possibilities will be affordable enough to be a powerful tool for the sharing of the Christian message, even as printing turned out to be a driving force for the Reformation of the 16th century. I will continue to look for signs that the churches are confronting this opportunity more energetically. The challenge for the "virtual church" will be to develop a way of feeding and healing in addition to presenting the traditional message. This may require a new breed of missionary. "The Virtual Missionary". The challenge will be to convert "zeros and ones" (binary code), into food, medicine, friendship and tangible help.

The principal tool for effective chaplaincy in our rapidly changing society is a comprehensive and exhaustive understanding of Critical Incident Stress and its wide-ranging effects upon those to whom we minister. Community Service Chaplains are professional or lay ministers who have observed the overwhelming need to minister to the community as a whole, as opposed to the sub-culture of people who bring their Christian values into the church.

The Community Service Chaplain sees the great need to go "beyond the gates"[4] of traditionalism and take the ministry of the church to those who do not enter the church. In essence, in accordance with the scripture, these Community Service Chaplains actually take ministry to Christ. Hebrews 13:12, 13. "Wherefore Jesus also, that he might sanctify the people with his own blood, suffered

---

[4] Favorite Chaplaincy Expression of Dr. Robert D. Crick, International Director of Church of God Chaplains Commission

without the gate. Let us go forth therefore unto him without the camp, bearing his reproach."

Chaplaincy has developed into a ministry of specialized disciplines over the past thirty-five years. However, during that thirty-five year period, pitifully little has been written regarding the actual accomplishment of chaplaincy ministries, with the understandable exception of Military Chaplains. Recently hospital, clinic and prison chaplaincy is being given more and more exposure.

What appears to be needed are some definitive tools which will assist ministers to perform multiple ministry tasks which are not specifically directed to pulpit ministry or those tasks which are most often understood as pastoral by nature.

On a personal note...

Shortly after my conversion to Christ in 1969, the Holy Spirit called me into the ministry during a Church of God Camp meeting in Kaiserslautern, West Germany. I had been struggling with the call, not so much because of the "call" itself, but rather, several of my close friends had received the call of God, and I did not want to give the appearance of "following the crowd" or to have the calling appear less sacred, because it was the "in thing" for young converts. I did receive the call of God and announced it to my pastor and friends; however, there was a caveat. I was to minister overseas and that is where I spent the next 17 years – on the foreign mission field. My family and I had no idea, at the time, how well this would prepare me for community service ministry upon my return to the USA.

It would not be until returning to the United States that I would realize a very specific direction that the Lord would take me. I would soon engage myself in a full time calling to Community Service Chaplaincy. In tandem with the pastorate, this ministry has opened up doors of opportunity that were never in my wildest dreams.

Acceptance of Chaplaincy Role

During my time as missionary in Italy I began to receive several calls from the US Government to volunteer my services to our servicemen in Italy. I was, on a number of occasions, loaded onto a Navy cargo plane and flown to different destinations in Italy to offer Divine Worship and to give counsel to United States military personnel in Italy.

Later while serving a missionary post in Germany, I was contracted by the US Army as a chaplain to serve the needs of soldiers and airmen. After returning to the States in 1986 I was called upon by the local chief of police to offer assistance to officers and staff who were struggling with personal and family issues. It was at this point in my pastoral and ministry vocation that I realized that God was truly taking me in a different ministry direction, other than the traditional. Eventually I was drafted into the ranks of the Federal Bureau of Investigation, to assist in the establishment of a nationwide chaplaincy program. This will be addressed more at length later in the book.

Commitment to writing this book as a training manual.

As ministry involvement became more directed to non-traditional ministry the author saw the need to establish some personal guidelines as well as direction for others who might choose to follow a similar path that he had done. During his work with the FBI, he had served principally as a counselor and spiritual advisor, but the longer he served he was called upon to give various forms of instruction to the staff and especially to new chaplains coming on board. It was evident that a teaching aid or manual was necessary. Additionally, the author was being asked to train police, hospital and prison chaplains for different agencies. The instruction became so comprehensive that it was obvious that the training could fit into most, if not all, market place ministry situations. Thus began work on an overall manual in 1993 and completed it in 1996. It is now in its 15th edition, with many refinements, redactions and deletions thanks to other Community Service Chaplains with a vision for ministry beyond the walls of the traditional church. Consequently, the work on the manual and many instructive seminars has been the impetus for this book.

Methods, approaches, resources and tools

A variety of methods are used in the development of this book. Trending toward the practical aspect of research, there is a heavy reliance upon sources that have actually "been there, and done that", especially regarding actual case studies and empirical data.

Other methods and approaches has been the utilization of non-published information gathered by colleagues in various fields of chaplaincy, such as prison, hospital and law enforcement, to name of few. This data will range from western social norms such as North America and Western Europe, to more Eastern European and Pacific Asian models.

Many of the resources that were used in this writing come from pastors, ministers and laity who are working in market place type ministries as an extension of their pulpit/traditional ministries.

Certain Expected Results

Throughout the research and writing of this book, the author has fully expected to develop a comprehensive model in written format for chaplaincy outreach to the community that addressed contemporary social focus and areas of Crisis. It is a goal of this book to provide a tool of instructions and guidance manual specifically for advanced chaplains to be able to identify and intervene in their community where social needs and crisis events are present. Hopefully, this book will provide a novice chaplain the necessary information for explaining to a secular agency the need for chaplaincy. This will include the legalities of the chaplaincy and the financial savings to community organization or agency to integrate such a program (ministry) into their organization, agency or department.

This book, along with the Community Service Chaplaincy training manuals can give a prospective employer or agency director the comfort necessary to engage a essentially trained clergy person or faith leader in the ministry of chaplaincy.

Possible impact of this project

The author trusts by defining the varied characteristics of chaplaincy ministry, that it will open a broader door of ministry for the active pastor. Many ministers are leaving the ministry prematurely due to many factors, which will be outlined in the body of the book. As a result of this attrition, this book can assist ministers and pastors to re-direct their ministry in such a way to gain fulfillment in an area that is not seen or understood in the traditional sense.

I look for this book to be utilized by various chaplaincy-training organizations as part of their mandatory chaplaincy tract of study. The chaplain, especially the chaplain in support of the community or volunteer chaplain will need to have a mission statement to adequately articulate his/her goal outside of the church setting. As will be mentioned later in the book, the chaplain must be able to define his/her ministry or someone else will do it for the chaplain. Therefore, as part of the definition of chaplaincy ministry, we will look at the following mission statement as a model.

Mission Statement of the Community Service Chaplain

The Mission of any Community Service Chaplain's program is to anticipate and respond to the need for emotional and spiritual guidance and assistance in time of personal or collective crisis among employees and agencies being served by Community Service Chaplains.

The Community Service Chaplain is actively committed to enriching the lives of the people he/she serves by providing emotional and spiritual guidance, which is necessary for daily living and an effective work environment.

The Community Service Chaplain fosters an atmosphere of trust and confidentiality for the employees of each agency or firm being served and the chaplain is pledged to the protection of each employee's privacy and confidence. By providing resources for emotional and spiritual health and personal development, the Community Service Chaplain helps in strengthening the entire work force family.

Community Service Chaplains are men and women of various ministerial and professional backgrounds who are dedicated to the spiritual, emotional and physical well being of the employees of the occupational field wherein they are called to minister. A Community Service Chaplain is trained in areas of counseling, human behavior, pastoral care and/or other related areas.

Community Service Chaplains are resources for stress management, critical incident stress debriefings, emotional disorders, marriage and family counseling, grief and depression disorders, and spiritual guidance when called upon. Community Service Chaplains are available on a volunteer basis to offer their services and find resources where possible to meet the needs of employees and their family.

The Community Service Chaplains understand their role to be that of service and contribution. Anything other than commitment to service and contributing to the community or organization cannot truly be seen as a significant involvement with society at large. Chaplains are to render service to the men and women of the organization being served. Additionally the Chaplains are to give service to the Church, which recognizes the need to minister in the market place and service to our Lord and Savior Jesus Christ. The contribution of each chaplain is that of his/her time, talents, care, professional expertise and often, their personal resources. This is to be done with a genuine love for those who serve our communities and citizens.

Philosophy and Role of the Community Service Chaplain

Philosophically, Community Service Chaplains will enter the community as a servant of the Lord and of the agency to which they may attach themselves. As Chaplains, we understand ideally, that we wish to promote the Kingdom of God and fulfill the Great Commission. It must be understood, however, that the CSC should not attempt to become THE pastor to the members of the workplace. There are many Godly and conscientious Christians who are already committed to their local church and denomination, but the presence of a Chaplain in their workplace can serve as a calming and healing agent in time of crisis. As a CSC you will be a valuable resource and minister for them, but our philosophy and role is NOT to build our own kingdom, but rather the Kingdom of God. The Chaplain will no doubt find many employees who are both un-churched and without commitment to God. They will often look to the Chaplain as their own pastor as time passes or crisis develops in their life or family.

A philosophy of ministry must be established and implemented from the onset of any community service ministry. The writer has learned from many years of ministry outside the traditional walls of the church, that when ministering in the community, a definite ministry philosophy must be in place. If the chaplain does not define his\her own ministry, then they need be well assured that someone else will do if for them. For example, when I first entered community service as a law enforcement chaplain, one of the first mistakes that I made was to allow the officers, which I served, to give definition to the ministry. My vision of ministry was to be of aid and assistance in as many spiritual and practical ways as possible for the Law Enforcement personnel. I soon realize that while riding along with officers or attending to a domestic situation with the authorities, they soon developed their own conceptions of what my ministry was to be.

To some it was to help with children, to others, to give advice to parents of runaway children and yet to other officers, it was to get "the bad guy" saved after the officer arrested them. None of these things was part of the mission that I had envisioned for this ministry. So, I soon realized that I had to be able to articulate very clearly and very early in the ministry of community service just exactly what my role was to be. I would soon learn that great caution was to be taken regarding the chaplaincy, as it truly became a DISEASE of chaplaincy. Chaplaincy, like other diseases has a tremendous affect upon one's blood. Although I am speaking euphemistically, this ministry really does impact the minister in a way that the traditional ministry does not. There is often an emotional "rush or high" that is not often felt in ministry within the four walls of the traditional church.

Don't allow chaplaincy to become your weakness.

I would encourage all chaplains, and especially community service chaplains to be cautious about the use of statistics. This topic may seem unimportant at a time that a chaplain is instructing, assisting or ministering, but be assured it puts the chaplains integrity into focus. As I have continued for the past three decades to give instruction to various ministers such as pastors, chaplains, evangelists, etc. I have been able to see strengths and weaknesses among chaplains. One principal weakness I have notices is the lack of commitment to update necessary statistics. Personally I have had to make a conscientious decision to do this necessary research in order to maintain integrity with my own teaching and chaplaincy service.

Another weakness I have identified among community service chaplains is the over commitment to the implementation of practical chaplaincy – The difficulty that chaplains have in saying "no". There are several reasons for this. Chaplaincy is the type of ministry that is actually like a virus, once in the system, you cannot get rid of it. Another is that, unlike traditional ministry, where often the dynamics are predictable, the chaplaincy is very unpredictable. As a result, the pastor serving as a chaplain tends to "run" to the excitement of the need. Add to this, the psychological issues of a caregiver, you have a recipe for personal and family disaster. Regarding this issue of not being able to "say no", I have observed that Chaplains and many pastors also, can not say "no" except to their own family. This will become catastrophic.

There are a variety of issues that led me to write this book. Principally the overwhelming need for care and evangelism are the most compulsive issues that brought me to this. Other facts that came into "play" regarding my desire to write on the subject of Community Service Chaplaincy are a declining desire of the clergy to remain in a traditional pulpit ministry and the suffering of our communities with regard to suicide, domestic violence, and additionally, other social ills that are not being met with the spiritual dynamics that the church has at its disposal. I have observed over many years in chaplaincy, that the church has the manpower and the resources to minister directly to the community at large, but it does not have the training or "chaplaincy mentality"[5] to engage the community in ministry unless it is in an evangelistic role. Unfortunately

---

[5] Chaplains mentality should be the Samaritan Mentality, Jake Popejoy

this role of evangelization is acted out, by and large, inside the church and not on the streets of the marketplace. (What's wrong with this picture.) This is, in the opinion of the author, a result of not understanding the overwhelming need to provide "care" before evangelism.

Another dynamic that I have observed and studied, which necessitated the writing of this book, is the obvious fact that many ministers and strong laymen find it difficult to minister outside the church. My belief of this hypothesis is that most clergy and church caregivers have found a zone of comfort in the church. In the marketplace, a minister's comfort level is constantly being challenged. This challenge result from threats to traditional doctrinal positions, lack of education on behalf of the minister or chaplain, and even the pastor or chaplain's own insecurities about their calling.

Community Service Chaplains, will learn very rapidly that they should become sociologists and as well as caregivers and theologians. While it is essential to adopt a mental and spiritual direction of care, which is to precede evangelism, it is imperative to grasp the dynamics of societal responses to crisis, needs and spiritual perceptions, and even to the care, which the chaplain offers.

In essence this book will be two fold in its nature. It will address training and "calling" issues of the chaplain. Additionally, it will focus on understanding the dynamics and effects of societal crises and stresses. Without the blending of these two, the ministry of the Community Service Chaplain will be hobbled if not totally rendered impotent.

The Abuse of Power as a Chaplain

Most men and women who enter into the Community Service Chaplaincy enter for the noble and Godly purpose of service, and to contribute to the fulfilling of the Great Commission. *Matthew 28:18-ff. And Jesus came and spake unto them, saying, "All power is given unto me in heaven and in earth. Go ye therefore, and teach all nations, baptizing them in the name of the Father, and of the Son, and of the Holy Ghost: Teaching them to observe all things whatsoever I have commanded you: and, lo, I am with you alway, even unto the end of the world. Amen".* Consequently, the CSC does not think of him/herself as a powerful person apart from the spiritual sense. In point of fact, the Community Service Chaplain will quickly learn that he/she wields a large amount of power.

The employers will soon learn that their employees trust and confide in the chaplain. This means that the chaplain may know what the employee thinks of his/her employer, be it bad or good. This is information, which many employers would like to know. The dilemma for the chaplain is obvious. He or she has a potential opportunity to "please" the boss at the expense of this confided knowledge. Be well aware this will happen to all community service chaplains who exercise or display leadership during their ministry.

The author's first experience as a Community Service Chaplain serving a small city police department was a learning experience in power. Although this chaplain's service was to the police department, the mayor of the city called for a conference. At the conference, the mayor informed the chaplain that it would be the responsibility of the chaplain to "inform" the mayor of any unusual behavior by any member of the police department to include the administrative staff. In essence, the chaplain was being asked to be a city or departmental spy. It is important to know that from the Mayor's point of view, this was an acceptable request, because He, the mayor, was in essence approving of the position of the chaplain. I informed the mayor that, in my opinion, this would undermine that actual purpose of the ministry and that I would be ineffective as a community servant. After more explanation to the mayor, nothing else was ever said about the Mayor's request and confidentiality was maintained.

The Chaplain's perceived authority

Another problem, which exists, is that the chaplain will almost always be seen as an authority figure. The reason is that chaplains normally have an open door to the administration, which will include the supervisors, section leaders, foremen, directors and even CEOs. Hence, the chaplain's "privilege of access" can be misinterpreted by the rank and file as "authority". This is however, only "perceived authority". The bosses know this and the chaplain knows this, but to others, it is viewed as a position of command. The Community Service Chaplain will be in a position to do things just because of the perceived authority. This is an awesome responsibility that the chaplain must carry very righteously. Once abused, it can become as addicting as any other type of power.

There are two important things to note.

The chaplain indirectly represents all other chaplains. Do not jeopardize the integrity and reputation of other chaplains because of your lack of discretion or integrity.

The presence of an "expert" authority such as the chaplain can influence individuals to engage in acts they normally would not consider. The chaplain is often seen as part of the administration and therefore the perception of many employees and Emergency Service Persons is that the chaplain is a person of power in the "system". In most cases this not all true. But often, this false perception is often appealing to the chaplain. It may give the chaplain a sense of power or be an ego builder.

The danger in this false perception is that the employees will sometimes expect the chaplain to "fix" something for them in a time of personal need. The end result of this is that the employ potentially loses faith in the chaplain, the agency or both.

Thinking like a chaplain

In the course of Chaplaincy ministry there will be a temptation to respond to most situations in a manner that is consistent with good pastoral care. This of course is not a bad thing when attempting to be a caregiver or shepherd. There is a problem, however, with this "good" that one attempts to do. For pastors who have been in the ministry for several years, many problems that the pastor faces are recurring problems. Often the answer to these recurring problems becomes something like a mathematical equation. Two plus two is four and the answer never changes. This is often because we tend to minister to people who have a similar belief system or theology as the pastor or caregiver.

In Chaplaincy, the answer will sometimes change because of the context and belief systems of the people to whom we minister. Whether we like it or not, chaplaincy can be and often is vastly different from pastoral ministry. Therefore it is incumbent upon the Community Service Chaplain to begin "thinking like a chaplain and not exclusively like a pastor".

The Community Service Chaplain who has not yet learned to "think" like a chaplain will continually be tempted to re-tool another's theology. During counseling a person will use inappropriate language or make an anti-faith statement, and without due care, the chaplain may immediate begin to devise a way to get this person to "think like me". Failure of ministry is sure to follow.

Pastors often have a compelling urge to "fix things". This may be a result of seemingly always having a good spiritual answer for the problems of the parish. The chaplain must learn to accept the fact about workplace problems. "They are what they are, and not what WE want them to be".

Pastors and other caregivers enter into Community Service Chaplaincy with pre-defined perceptions of Crisis. These perceptions have generally resulted from the type of ministry in which they have historically been engaged. Some examples will follow.

A pastor may see anything that disrupts the continuity of his/her vision for the church as a crisis. We tend to be able to handle the Status Quo, but when this is disturbed, we may perceive it as a crisis.

A career missionary may perceive the loss of a long-term financial donor, or the loss of a ministry team member as a crisis.

A youth pastor may perceive an intense and heated argument with the elders of the church or an argument with parents of teenagers to be a crisis.

The bus ministry pastor may perceive the rejection of his/her annual budget request for repairs or for an additional bus as a crisis.

Much of the above is a form of pastoral thinking. We are creatures of faith, so we think most people have a faith and when we enter the market place and begin to minister to people who have no faith system nor do they want one, this is extraordinarily foreign to us. We must learn and refine a chaplaincy thinking process in order to be productive in community service ministry.

Coming of Age – The Chaplain and Chaplaincy finding their place.

It is imperative that Community Service Chaplaincy must be understood and defined as a theology of practical sociology. If a pastor or faith leader only interprets or defines chaplaincy as a spiritual dynamic, he or she is bound to fail in this ministry, which by its nature is called to reach society "where they are".

It is the writer's opinion that the "Good Samaritan" was in point of fact the first historically recorded chaplain of the New Testament era. He encounters a man on the Jericho road. This man was bleeding and dying. The Samaritan new relatively nothing about this man, yet he "came where he was: and when he saw him, he had compassion on him, and went to him"[6]

This is the implementation of the sociology of Christ. There was no concern as to whether the man was a robber himself, a sexual deviant, an alcohol or drug addict. No, the Samaritan rendered help only because the man was hurting. Unfortunately the church of the 21st century is not always as pure with its care giving. Pastors are as guilty of this as the person setting on the pew. The chaplain cannot be guilty of selective care.

As Christ did, the chaplain feeds people, not because they are potential church members, but rather, we feed people because they are hungry. In the story of the Good Samaritan, we see the concerns of Christ as sociological.

---

[6] Luke 10:33, 34, Holy Bible, KJV

This does not dismiss in any way the necessary spiritual dynamic, but rather integrates practical sociology into the theology, which Christ instructed. He looks at people in there completeness

A continued reference to conceptualism is vital for the chaplain to understand care ministry and helping people in their pain. The relationship that a Community Service Chaplain establishes with those to whom he/she ministers gives the chaplain a means to see their past, understand their present and assist them in shaping their future. The fears, faith and hopes of the parishioner or employee are all part of the spiritual context that the chaplain discovers.

The chaplain is able to minister, as did the Good Samaritan to the still bleeding wounds of the spiritually, physically and emotionally injured. The means of getting the best result for this ministry investment is to except with reservation that care must precede evangelism. It is certainly imperative to care for people within the gates of the traditional church, but equally important, if not more so, to care for those outside the gates, as Christ Himself did.

This brings us to a question that we must ask ourselves as ministers and chaplains. Exactly where IS Christ ministering today? Anton Boisen suggests to us *"Jesus visits our churches on Sunday, but has permanent residency with the homeless, the mentally ill and those in prison."* The point being, if we are to act in the name of Christ, and deliver the message that He died for, we must also go to places that Christ Himself would go. These places certainly may not be comfortable for traditional ministries, but nonetheless there are places far from the church where people are hurting.

When we are ministering in an unfamiliar world, other than that which we have grown comfortable, it is with certainty that our understanding of the world will develop and cause change within us.   As we develop this care ministry we are able to comprehend that care can be articulated in three dimensions. The three dimension of a caring ministry are Faith, Love and Hope.

- Faith – This is the dimension of covenant. As Chaplains we share our faith and assist people in either finding or developing a faith within themselves.

A shared faith is a special covenant, which represents a deep fidelity to God and the community, which we serve. It is a treaty of spiritual connection and application of a practical sociological theology.   For example, care for the hurting. This praxis is of course always found in the Father's love. He is always there, He always loves and He is always caring and He is always waiting for an opportunity to minister to us.

- Love – This is the dimension of Character. John Wesley identified Holiness itself as Love. The character of the chaplain is bound to the community in this dimension.

Love is compelling in and of itself, because the Scripture informs us that God is Love.[7] But the sharing of love or the sharing of God requires a person of noble character. Character has been defined by Merriam-Webster Online Dictionary as *"moral excellence and firmness."* Therefore, we are to understand why we do things, what is

---

[7] 1 Jo 4:8 - He that loveth not knoweth not God; for God is love. Holy Bible, KJV

the spiritual dynamic involved, is it love, selfishness, pride, egoism, and finally what is the expected result? Are we actually caring for the sake of the hurting or do we see an earthly or even heavenly reward in our endeavors. The answer to these questions, will help us define our Love, or Character. Finally, we will learn our Crisis depth. Through commitment to Love, the chaplain will soon understand the ramifications of Chaplaincy ministry. He or she will quickly determine if they are ministering out of their depth or if they are "in over their heads".

- Hope – This is the dimension of Commission

There is no doubt that the Community Service Chaplain as well as other clergy is ministering to a wounded church in a wounded world. One can never lose sight of the fact that the Church is and will ever remain the Bride of

Christ, yet irrefutably the church, herself, is wounded and hurting. The element that carries the church past her own pain and wounds is the Hope or Commission, which was given to us by Christ. We have a task that must be completed. In giving the hurting hope, we are able to endure our own suffering. Christ, as our example, demonstrated the presence of Joy that could be found in suffering. *Looking unto Jesus the author and finisher of our faith; who for the joy that was set before him endured the cross... "*[8]

To share this hope, requires the seizing of "optimal moments". Dr. Robert Crick, who served as International Director of the Church of God Chaplain's Commission, teaches in his Case Studies class at the Pentecostal Theological Seminary that there are optimal moments in the

[8] Heb 12:2, Holy Bible, KJV

lives of all of us. Especially as Christians, we need learn to identify, seize and reflect upon these moments. There must be a commitment, even a requirement for the Chaplain to move with God in response to these optimal moments. For the writer, one of these optimal moments was certainly the marrying of my wife. It absolutely could be no other. Not because I was not capable of feelings for another, or that my marriage was "made in heaven", but because, this woman, I knew, would follow me anywhere and be content with the little which I would be able to offer her. A second optimal moment for me would be the time that I agreed to contract with the Federal Bureau of Investigation. This course of action, this optimal moment, would continue to open doors of ministry to me that I cannot otherwise believe would have opened.

At the root of these three dimensions of care is the overwhelming fact that care must of necessity be radical. If care is not to be radical it will never change context. It will never have a different vision than that which it employs in our present ministry. It has been said of Albert Einstein, that he stated, "If a person does the same thing over and over again, yet he expects a different result each time, the poor person must have mental problems". For the Community Service Chaplain, care takes on a different face from the traditional. It may be seen as radical, but then so was the ministry of Jesus.

As I conclude this section of the book, I am reminded that as a Community Service Chaplain I have learned a very valuable and theological lesson about the dynamics of God's ministry. It is clear from the scripture that God does not love sin. He hates sin. But, by the very nature of God, which is Omnipresence, He always has to be in a sinful presence, (or He would not be omnipresent). He always has to be with people whether He hates to be or not. At first read, this may sound strange or even silly, but it has a powerful point to it. Even if God does not wish to be near someone who is continually doing sinful things and exploiting the innocent, He has to be, because of His nature.

If I do not wish to be near prostitutes, I don't go where they are. If I do not wish to be in contact with drug addicts or alcoholics, I simply avoid them. If I do not want to be anywhere near the perversion of child molesters, spouse abusers or pornographers, I simply stay away from them. God has a problem. He always has to be where they are. But, even with this inability to extract Himself from the presence of this horrible sin, He manifests His love by healing their broken hearts and waiting, in their sinful presence for their repentance. To minister in the fashion of Christ, we too, must go to uncomfortable places, "outside the gates".

Understanding the motives that help or hinder appropriate considerations of behavior in our society.

A powerful tool available for the Community Service Chaplain is to learn to grasp the motivations of social order in our cultures and subcultures. We must learn the answer to the question, "why do people do what they do?" As we search for these answers we identify motivations. Are people stimulated from internal motivations or external? When we study the people to whom we minister and for which these answers are applicable, we gain another valuable stratagem of ministry.

We soon discover that as we learn the motivational stimuli of those to whom we minister, we are also able to see the motivations as predictors to behavior. Consequently, we are able to help the parishioner or employee to "head off" some inevitable problems, which lie ahead. For example, if an individual's behavior is motivated by money or financial benefits, then of course he/she will tend to prioritize his/her time and affections to those things which will bring about the desired response. Hence, they can be likely to dedicate less time to family and friends which do not necessarily provide the financial return that is the prime motivator of this individual's behavior. A pastor or chaplain equipped with this knowledge can surely render assistance to the person when crisis comes to the family, or when the individual doesn't seem to understand why they are so often lonely and "misunderstood".

Within the topic of understanding the motives, which help or hinder behavior in our society are the myths of the ministry and the function of the ministry in society. Historically there have been many myths of the ministry perpetrated on society to include such things as ethical and moral behavior, responsibility, and discipline, just to name a few.

Myths themselves can be motivational. Myths often develop from a system of belief in the "teller" of a particular account. Even if the account is inaccurate, it will be believed if presented from a position of authority and respect. As a result myths about the ministry or the clergy themselves are often created from a belief in the person telling the story. In the following personal account, I found myself perpetuating a myth about ministerial behavior.

Shortly after my conversion I was called to the preaching ministry. I was converted through the efforts of the denomination of which I am still faithfully serving. My role models principally came from this church, which at the time of my conversion was ultra conservative. No jewelry was permitted, no cosmetics, no short pants for men or women, no movies, no attendance at sporting events, ad infinitum. I had accepted this as a "holy" lifestyle and intended to live it accordingly. On one occasion, my pastor, whom I dearly love, was preaching a sermon on the importance of the personal witness. Rather than address issues of personal soul winning, the pastor began to address proper attire for the soul winner.

He continued to preach on the importance of an appropriately dressed minister of the Gospel. In the course of his message, he made a point to say that a preacher should be "instant in season and out of season"[9]. Of course he used the II Timothy passage to demonstrate the Biblical authority for what he was going to employ. He proceeded to instruct the young ministers that a pastor should always wear a long sleeved shirt, a tie and of course, a coat when possible. The myth had begun, or at least I was perpetuating the myth that had, no doubt, also been handed to my pastor.

For the next five years, almost every day of my life, I wore a coat and tie. Of course there is absolutely nothing wrong with wearing this clothing, except I found myself, mowing the grass with a long sleeved shirt and tie. I picked apples from our fruit trees with the awareness that I must be "instant in season and out of season". And for me, the most ridiculous behavior was to change the oil in my car dressed

---

[9] 2 Timothy 4:2 Preach the word; be instant in season, out of season; reprove, rebuke, exhort with all longsuffering and doctrine. – Holy Bible, KJV

as if prepared for a hospital visit. Unfortunately, I carried this myth for five full years.

There are numerous other myths that have been perpetrated on our society. In fact so many, that I could not address them in this short book, but among others is the myth that it is "lonely at the top". Unfortunately, people are lonely at the top, not because it is the fault of ministry, but rather, because the ministers won't take others to the top with them. All too often pastors and occasionally chaplains are taught that intimacy becomes a stumbling block to ministry. As a young pastor, I was told by a number of my colleagues and mentors that I should not get "too close" to the congregation. If I got "too close" to them, I might not be able to ministry without partiality. Fortunately, I learned early in ministry that this was a myth, or in laymen's terms, a load of rubbish.

When a pastor or chaplain accepts these myths and perpetuates them, they (the pastors), contribute to the motives that hinder sound societal behavior with regard to the mission of the church and Community Service Chaplaincy. The final myth, which I will mention, is with regard to "calling". For the clergy to promulgate the myth, that they alone have a call of God is both, inconsistent with the scriptural directive of the priesthood of all believers, and the imperative of the Great Commission.[10] Although, I have never heard it directly said from the pulpit, the pulpit allows the myth to continue when laity does not except a calling for their lives. If a person is a house painter, they should, seek God and know, that this is what God wants them to be,

---

[10] Matthew 28:19, Go ye therefore, and teach all nations, baptizing them in the name of the Father, and of the Son, and of the Holy Ghost:, Holy Bible, KJV

rather than painting only for the sake of occupational security.

Community Service Chaplains should get a firm grip and understanding of myths and how these myths have the potential for altering or shaping behavior in our society.

The chaplain's role in society is still not clearly defined. Although Chaplains have been with us for several hundred years, by and large, it appears that the general understanding of the public, with regard to chaplaincy, is that of a Military Officer who "ministers" to the troops. A second generalization is that a chaplain is one who serves in a highly institutionalized environment such as a hospital or prison. While both of the aforementioned characterizations are correct, they are incomplete and do not provide a definition of chaplaincy.

There appears to be very little writing done on the role and ministry of the chaplain. That is, with the exception of a legion of articles and presentations within the bounds of military chaplaincy. Although hospital and corrections chaplaincies are evolving and gaining greater acceptance, the amount of information available is paltry compared to the military chaplaincy. This is most probably a result of the age of the institution, i.e., the military. As far back as the Book of Deuteronomy, armies have been taking their "priests" into battle and service. The short history of other institutions, such as hospitals and prisons, may give some insight as to the slow evolution of the chaplaincy into more modern agencies.

A further goal therefore, of this book, is to raise the awareness of the readers that the role of the chaplain needs to be elevated to a more prominent and contemporary state of ministry.   Ministry, albeit, that is not definable by conventional measures, but rather, a ministry that plumbs the depths of issues that are not often brought into the traditional church. The Chaplaincy has yet to "come of age". I believe that we will see this ministry rapidly maturing as we continue into the 21st century with the fears of terrorism, secularism and nebulous pluralism in our schools and college campuses.

What makes the chaplain do what he or she does? Earlier research done by behavioral scientists have determined several characteristics which emergency service care givers have in common, at the very least, they share a large percentage of these common characteristics. Over the past 30 years of my chaplaincy ministries, both through research and observation, I have concluded the following characteristics which are found in emergency service persons are also to be found in Community Service Chaplains.

A list with short definitions of the characteristics of Emergency Service Persons is to follow. The value of this finding and knowledge lies in the awareness that if a Community Service Chaplain understands the dynamics of these characteristics, they become a valuable tool in ministering to various community agencies. Therefore, if one knows "why an individual does what he/she does, then a tool is provided for insight to family, marital, spiritual and authority related problems.

However, before moving into the next topic, I wish to address the issue of dealing with crisis and problems in a sub-culture. In our world, sub-cultures are often viewed through the lenses of race, sexual orientation, color, and often religion. In our recent politically correct society, we are, in fact, attempting to do away with, or at the very least, subdue sub-cultures. To do this, political correctness is asking our society to embrace and assimilate into the sub-cultures, rather than the sub-cultures embracing and assimilating into the larger society. If eradication of sub-cultures becomes largely successful, then morals, behaviors and values come under assault. Consequently, the development of new definitions of morality, lifestyle and even new definitions of crises will change the way that pastors and chaplain's minister to the community.

To the chaplain, sociologist and behavioral scientist, the understanding of sub-cultures is imperative for appropriate community service ministry and crisis intervention. Following is an example of crisis in subcultures.

- Two men in the United States are driving to work on any given day. One of the men, 34 years old, is born and raised in Texas. He happens to be a white American citizen. The American citizen has a car accident on his way to work. No injuries were involved. The police arrive on the scene, proof of insurance, drivers license and registration are all requested. All the above is made available and all is in order. The accident results in the possibility of insurance litigation and of course a delay to work.

- The other person involved is approximately the same age, but is born and raised in Mexico and is presently an undocumented immigrant to the USA. He too, has an accident on the way to work. No injuries were involved. Now the scenario changes with the Mexican. Because of his undocumented status, he may feel panic and act irrationally, such as flee the scene to avoid police involvement. Another option is that he stays and waits for the police. The police arrive. Proof of insurance, registration and drivers license is all requested. None of these, or only part of these is available because of his undocumented status. The results of this accident can be court fines, confiscation of the vehicle, some time in jail or even all of the above.

So what we have is two men, both hard workers and on the way to their respective jobs. But the chaplain has to consider the sub-cultures of the men. The Mexican is a member of a sub-culture of the greater whole of the USA, but this particular person is also a member of the "undocumented" sub-culture which brings a whole set of crisis issues to the man involved.

Why Does the Emergency Services Person do what he/she does?

Very much like police officers, firemen and hospital emergency room staff, pastors and Community Service Chaplains, fall into the category of Emergency Services

Persons. To successfully and appropriately minister to the diverse genre of the community, the chaplain should have a keenly good idea of what motivates this community. If the chaplain is unaware of the stimuli, which motivate these caregivers, the chaplain loses, or at the very least, ignores a powerful tool with which to respond to their needs whether on the job, off duty or in their homes.

Following is a list of factors with which the community service chaplain should familiarize him/herself. These factors are general characteristics and traits, and of course will vary person to person. Every caregiver will be different, yet most emergency service people will possess a large portion of these characteristics. While this list is certainly not exhaustive, it will give the chaplain an advantage that he/she might not normally have without this understanding.

It cannot be emphasized enough that this book is a resource of tools. Each item brought to the attention of the reader should be considered as a tool, not for display, but rather for use. When the pastor begins seeing the sociological implications of the tools at his/her disposition, then the pastor begins thinking on a different plane. It is important that the pastor maintain a strong theology, but likewise understand that each individual to whom the pastor/chaplain ministers, has a specific context and background, that is peculiar to the individual. If the pastor interprets the needs of people strictly from his/her own biblical foundation, there will be something valuable missed in the ministry opportunity. That which is missed is the establishment of a relationship with the individual, based on the historical context and psychological baggage that the person brings to the relationship. Without understanding the sociological ramifications to each relationship, the pastor is tempted to give "broad brushed" answers to desperate problems. Answers such as, "well now, we must pray about this", "God has everything under control". While these answers are often acceptable in the routine of traditional church dynamics, how can we expect such answers to apply to people who are non-believers or atheistic in spiritual persuasion? We cannot. Yet, it is our responsibility to minister to those in need. We must address the question, why did Jesus feed the multitudes? Was it to gain popularity? Was it to gain their tithes and offerings or church membership? Was it to demonstrate His closeness to the heavenly Father? No! He fed the multitude because they were hungry. Therefore, we as ministers, pastors and chaplains, we care because there is pain. Following is a brief list of characteristics of both emergency service people, and caregivers, to whom we as chaplains will have an opportunity to minister.

Obsessive/Compulsive, Controller

This characteristic is presented in a very loose and broad sense, insomuch that the author is not insinuating a mental or psychological disorder, but rather a temperament. There are many things that motivate an Emergency Service Person or caregiver to do the things that he or she does, and among them are the issues of compulsion and control. While these characteristics are not often thought of in positive ways, it still must be understood that this is often a driving force which allows the Emergency Service Person or caregiver to effectively accomplish their tasks.

By way of example, a police officer, generally wants to do things "right", and they are not often happy until things are done to their own satisfaction. When working in an environment, where these characteristics are prominent among the majority of the employees, the possibility of explosive outbursts and utterances of dissatisfaction will be regularly experienced. While the Emergency Service Person will be governed and "disciplined" by certain departmental and agency policies, an alert chaplain will readily understand that the "home front" does not have such regulating policies. It is there, at home, that the officers will find themselves most challenged to be understanding and tolerant. Unfortunately this is not often done and trouble is not far behind.

Take notice, the very temperament or characteristics, which make the Emergency Service Person superbly good at their, job, can be the same characteristics that potentially spell disaster at home or in other non-work related environments. The Emergency Services Person, or caregiver uses this characteristic to "get the job done" while in the work place, and then, even sub-consciously, brings these characteristics to the home. When the ESP, does not get the same result that he/she gets on the job, it can be interpreted as lack of respect, rebellion, or some other factor that immediately brings an aggressive confrontation into the home.

The Emergency Service Person does not always have the training or skill to identify that this is a hazard of the job. The Emergency Service Person has a workplace "voice" that is often used to project power and authority. When this voice is brought into the home, simply for the purpose of obtaining compliance from children or spouse, it is seen as abusive and out of order. The chaplain needs this understanding and awareness to minister to the needs of these valuable people.

Action Oriented Easily Bored

Emergency Service Personnel (ESP) and caregivers are, by and large, "action oriented", therefore they may often be perceived by the public and members of their families, as narrow minded and self-centered. The very nature of the Emergency Service Person and caregivers is one of protection and service. They feel that their service cannot be accomplished satisfactorily if they are not out in the midst of all that is happening. The Chaplain will note that many Emergency Service Persons are "four wheel drive" type of individuals, so even their off duty time demands that they be doing something exciting. Families aren't always equipped for or excited about this type of lifestyle for a daily diet. Consequently, families' feel their spouse or parent is disinterested in them, their interests, or even worse, they (the ESP) are more interested in other people. The dilemma, of course, is that the Emergency Service Person and Caregivers do not recognize this as a problem as they are focused and busy caring and protecting others.

The Emergency Service Person, especially, lives a life that involves regular adrenal rushes. Reliving the experience of the fire, the chase, the fight, or some other dangerous activity heightens the adrenal rush. The reliving is done through conversation and recounting of the events with their peers. The peer is often able to identify with the Emergency Service Person by contributing to the recounting of the event, asking the appropriate questions and using the appropriate nomenclature for occupational tools and devices. The Emergency Service Person renews the initial adrenal rush and their value to the community and the department, which they serve, is affirmed. The Emergency Service Person or caregiver cannot get the same satisfaction when recounting the event at home. The reason is often because the Emergency Service Person and caregiver attempts to shield or protect the family from his/her danger, or the ESP has learned from experience that the family doesn't appreciate the dynamics of the occupation and the "rush" is lost on the uninitiated.

With this knowledge, the Chaplain is better equipped to minister to the Emergency Service Person, the caregiver and his/her family during a time of family trauma or stress.

Therefore, this knowledge is a required tool for the Community Service Chaplain.

Risk Taker, Highly Dedicated

Obviously, risk comes with being a law enforcement officer, firefighter, emergency medical responder, Emergency Service Person and even a Caregiver. With this risk and dedication come several issues that are often confusing to the average ESP. They find it very difficult to understand and accept criticism as relates to their job. They cannot understand why others do not see the dangers or frustrations, which are inherent to their tasks, and in which they are often themselves, and this is for the sake of the very people who are criticizing.

A prime example of this aforementioned confusion is found in the case of the Trans World Airline flight # 800 which crashed of the coast of New York in the summer of 1996. Emergency Service People from all around the United States converged on this terrible scene, all of them offering help and assistance. Much of this assistance offered was voluntary, therefore causing a financial hardship on many of the Emergency Service Persons, but yet they came. During the course of the recovery of the 232 bodies that were lost in the crash, many of the family members of the victims brought into question the quality of work, the slow pace of the recovery and the earnestness of the Emergency Service Persons. Of course, the families of the deceased were suffering and grieving, and did not understand the dynamics of the recovery. They just wanted their loved ones recovered.

The criticisms of many of the family members found their way into the media, some into print, and others onto radio and television. The Emergency Service Persons, working so diligently, heard these criticisms, and became angry and even cynical about the media and even the grievers. The fact was that the Emergency Service Persons were doing their absolute best, and at great risk to their own personal safety, to serve the very people who were criticizing them. This case will be further discussed under a later topic.

(*Strong need to be needed*).

Another problem comes directly from the family. Spouses and children will question why the officer or emergency caregiver takes certain risks, (gunshots, fires, disease). The family may actually become angry with the Emergency Service Person when he/she takes risks. This stems from one of the Five Fears of Intimacy[11], which will be discussed later in the book. The anger is attributed to their love and need of security. The ESP often interprets this as selfishness on behalf of his family and is seen as resentment the family may harbor toward the ESP's job. An additional issue that the Community Service Chaplain must consider is that pastors and chaplains also tend to be risk takers, but in somewhat different ways. It is not unusual for caregivers to engage in ´risk taking´ behavior. As an example, to care for the needs of parishioners, a pastor may place him or herself in a position of borderline impropriety. In order to identify with the emotional pain or distress that a parishioner is suffering, the pastor or chaplain gets closer and closer on an emotional plane and then on the physical. Sometimes this is even misinterpreted as a new ´spiritual

---

[11] Patricia Shehan, Veterans Hospital, Indianapolis, Indiana, USA

plane´. It is absolutely imperative that the pastor and/or the chaplain understand that risk taking behavior is not necessarily a behavior which puts one into physical danger, but rather a behavior that ultimately is destructive to the character, confidence and trust of those to whom he or she is ministering.

The author, having worked for several years as a Chaplain with the Federal Bureau of Investigation, has counseled FBI agents who found themselves with marital problems because of this type of behavior. While supporting the victim of a crime or a government witness, Agents have become so emotionally attached to their charges that this attachment soon transferred to inappropriate sexual behavior.

Strong need to be needed

The need to be needed is a very strong trait of the Emergency Services Personnel and Caregivers within their sub-cultural community. Satisfaction of a job "well done" is important to all. It is, however, an imperative for Emergency Services Persons such as the law enforcement officer, fire fighter, caregiver, etc. This "need" cannot always be met in the Emergency Service Persons family. Obviously, if it could be so, the ESP would be much healthier and happier. This "need to be needed" is such a driving force that it can interrupt the normal thought processes associated with morals and ethics. When this need is taken to an extreme, it can end in disaster for the Emergency Service Person, often as a result of unhealthy relationships that spring from the honorable assistance being offered by the emergency caregiver.

It is extremely important to understand that this "need to be needed" is directly related to how the Emergency Service Persons believe their job is being perceived by the agency for which they are employed or serving. If the Emergency Service Personnel believe that their job is valued and necessary to the community or society in general, then occupational or "ministry" fulfillment is achieved. If the ESP perceives unfair criticism or deprecation, then this "need to be needed" is left unfulfilled, even if the family members are highly supportive of the Emergency Services caregiver. Consequently, the family and friends tend to be alienated from ESP. Because they don't understand the internal dynamics of the caregiver, they interpret the actions of the ESP as confusing and distancing. Believing that there is nothing they can do to 'please' the caregiver, they tend to withhold positive input altogether. Following is further detail of a case study initially mentioned earlier in the paper.

CASE STUDY

In 1996 Trans World Airline flight, number 800, crashed in the Atlantic off the coast of New York, near Long Island. It is believed that 232 people perished in the crash. The author was, at that time, employed by the Federal Bureau of Investigation as a Chaplain and Crisis Counselor. One of the responsibilities of the Chaplain was to offer Critical Incident Stress Debriefing and to the Emergency Service Personnel at the recovery point of the crash. The vital key to recovery of the bodies and debris were the divers and support personnel from the many responding agencies. The writer was able to observed the dynamics of this strong "need to be needed" while giving counsel to some of these men and women who were part of the many diving and recovery teams.

The teams would board a boat that would take them to the crash site, which was located about ten miles off shore. The depth of the water at the crash site was approximately 120-130 feet. The divers made a single round trip each day during the recovery process. Arriving at the site at about 7:30 am, they would not return until about 6:00 pm in the evening.

Several problems began to arise that were not anticipated in advance. Such a tragedy, with so much publicity, both national and international had not been experienced until that time. The world was watching and consequently evaluating the recovery process. Family members of the deceased had arrived on the scene. Hundreds of news agencies had sent personnel to cover this tragedy. And the world watched as daily, the divers brought to the surface the remains of the victims.

Because of decompression and recompression problems, the divers were only allowed to make one dive to the ocean floor each day. Of course there were scores of divers, but the task before them was a mammoth task. The crash site covered an area of more than 9 square miles.

By way of illustration, I present the following example for this case study. As a member of the FBI debriefing team, the author was sent to this terrible crash site. The debriefing team worked rotating assignments from day to day. We rotated between the morgue, body recovery, evidence retrieval and investigations. During my tour of "body recovery", I was assigned to be on a diving platform with police and Navy divers. Because of the slow process of decompression, the procedure that was followed was to take approximately 10-12 divers per diving platform. A diver was only allowed to dive once a day, principally because of the depth of water involved, 130 feet. A diver was lowered into the water and descended approximately 33 feet, or one atmosphere of pressure. The diver would then remain at that depth for 6 minutes then descend another 33 feet, repeating this procedure until on the ocean floor. The diver was then permitted to "work" only 10 minutes on the ocean floor. The instructions to the diver were to recover a body, if possible, or collect a piece of the aircraft (evidence). If the diver recovered a body or body part, they returned to the buoy line and began their ascent, using the same procedure as the descent. Therefore, they could ascend 33 feet; there they must wait 6 minutes, in the dark, in the cold with a cadaver or body part tied to them. They ascended another 33 feet, waited 6 more minutes and repeated the procedure until they reached the top. At the surface, the diver and his findings would be placed aboard the diving platform and there he/she would wait the rest of the day. They would watch the bodies be brought to the surface, either having accomplished their own dive for the day, or watch in fearful anticipation of their turn to make such a terrible and awesome dive.

At the end of the day, they would return to their homes and family, often only to hear through news media public criticism of their actions. This, of course, contributes to the terrible stress and anxiety that these heroes had to endure.

The above-mentioned case is very typical of the heroic efforts and thought processes made by men and women in the Emergency Services and the Caregiver communities. If the pastor/chaplain is not, at the least, basically equipped to deal with this ´need to be needed´, he/she will stand at the bottom of an almost insurmountable mountain, unable to climb to a meaningful relationship with the people who need the chaplain the most.

Difficulty saying "no"

One of the greatest sources of stress and frustration is a person's inability to say no. Emergency Service People and caregivers are no less guilty. The problem with this phenomenon is that the ESP or caregiver rarely has difficulty saying no when it comes to issues with the family or in the home. The problem develops with their cases at work and their need to be needed by others. Commitments will be made for special assignments, overtime, extra shifts, undercover activities and a host of other job related issues. "Burn out" will inevitably result. This burn out will manifest itself in a variety of symptoms. The Emergency Service People and/or Caregivers will be subject to a "them and us" syndrome. This can result in anger toward family because of demands that they, the family rightly make upon the ESP's time. Hence, anxiety and panic attacks and depression can be the outcome.

The reason behind this "difficulty saying no", often stems from the misperception that if one says "no", he/she will either not be liked or that he/she will not be called upon again. C.S. Lewis wrote in his short Essay, "The Inner Ring", "It is a terrible thing to be asked to come into work on a Saturday afternoon, yet there is one thing worse, not to be asked at all."

Unfortunately this very characteristic is deeply rooted in the caregiver ministries such as pastoral care, benevolences and chaplaincy. There seems to be an unwritten law that if one is a pastor or caregiver, that the word "no" cannot be found in one's vocabulary. It seems to be understood that saying "yes" to everyone, is part of the job description. It is so ingrained into the ecclesiastical ethos that is brings unwarranted guilt to the caregiver or Emergency Service Person, if they do not respond to a request in the affirmative. Most chaplains and pastors have no idea how powerful, and how destructive this inability can be. The most regrettable aspect surrounding this characteristic is that the chaplain, caregiver or Emergency Service Person has very little difficulty saying "no" to his/her own family. This is often excused or passed over with thoughtless responses such as, "it's my job", "it's my calling", or "you knew what you were getting when you married me." Of course the kids didn't know!

Rescue personality

Like the police officer, Emergency Service Personnel and Caregivers generally wish to be in the "thick" of things. This is not always because they enjoy a good fight, stressful situation, or wish to wield power and authority. It is often a genuine desire to help, and to rescue those who cannot help themselves at a particular time in their life. There is however a fine line between the "Rescuer" and the "Messiah Complex". Once this line is crossed, the ESP will tend to feel a failure if they cannot meet the need of the person who calls upon them for help.

With this characteristic also comes the dilemma of not wanting to leave the task until it is finished. This is not always possible. Law Enforcement officers often engage in activities that are frequently protracted. Example: hostage situations, natural disasters, mass casualty incidents and other such situations, which demand a large number of officers over a prolonged period of time. Like wise, the Emergency Service Person will attempt to do the same thing, in order to achieve the goal of "success" with the person with the life problem. As a result the ESP or Caregiver will fatigue quickly. At this point they are often ordered home at the end of their shift. This combination of fatigue and receiving an order they don't wish to hear often results in a volatile situation.

Family oriented - verbally

Pastors, Chaplains, Police officers, Emergency Service Personnel and Caregivers are often the first to speak about the sanctity of the family. They believe the family unit to be vital to the community and the nation. Obviously this cannot be faulted in and of itself. Unfortunately police officers and other ESP are statistically among the highest to experience divorce. Most such community servants will remarry after the divorce and many will remarry almost immediately.

This "link" with the family is vital to their personality, yet it is almost always a verbal affirmation of the family rather than a lived out reality. The chaplain will be well advised to keep in mind that <u>the very thing, which makes the ESP good at what he or she does, is often the very thing which makes the ESP a failure at marriage and family.</u>

The chaplain is challenged to reflect upon this axiom because it is very fitting to the personality of most clergy and chaplains as well.

Driven by internal motivations

Regardless of the amount of status or authority, which is provided to an emergency service caregiver, it is generally internal motives that drive him/her to continue to do their job and to do it effectively. It is obvious that such caregivers are not highly paid. The benefits to civil service employees and church leaders are not particularly abundant, and yet men and women continue to take the risks, work the long hours, suffer ridicule from the press and public and generally work a job that is often thankless. For this reason, the chaplain must understand that the Emergency Service Person (ESP) is driven by internal motives and not external. Chaplains, like these ESP caregivers are likewise motivated to do what they do by internal motivations. Consequently, the Community Service Chaplain may spend an inordinate amount of time in their volunteer ministry because of a "job satisfaction" received in the volunteer work rather than in the paid pulpit ministry. The motive may be for prestige, it may be for the "thrill", or it may be to be able (in the case of police) to carry a gun. The reality of the matter is this; when asked why they do it, most caregivers respond that they "want to make a difference" in their community. For example, the police officer has the opportunity to make some "wrongs" right. They have the opportunity to contribute in ways that others are unable. They actually have a pastor's heart.

Generally has a high tolerance for stress

Stress is a daily part of the ESP and Caregivers life and routine. Police officers have, like other emergency services persons, a high tolerance for stress. The Community Service Chaplain must not misinterpret this. Because the Emergency Service Person has a high tolerance, does not mean he/she is immune or can tolerate stress away from their job. This high tolerance is relative to the job. There are many officers and caregivers, who take the work home with them. In so doing, they are subject to "venting" their stress on their families. Additionally, because the ESP's characteristic is to have high tolerance for stress, the chaplain must all the more encourage these dedicated people to exercise, diet properly and take other necessary steps to buffer stress.

Generally has a high tolerance for anxiety

Finally, police officers, firefighters, and other caregivers have a high tolerance for anxiety. An officer is trained to treat the public with a certain demeanor. He/she is taught to remain in control of the situation. If they ever lose control, someone will most certainly get hurt. Because of this training, when an officer is experiencing mild anxiety, they learn to "maintain" control at all costs. They learn to tolerate certain things which others would not be able to tolerate. This is where the stress management axiom of "pay me now or pay me later" comes into play. The officer will only be able to maintain for so long without having to pay a physiological, even emotional cost. The physiological cost will manifest itself in symptoms that effect the emotions, behavior, cognition and physical systems of the body.

With regard to "pay me now or pay me later", it has long been know that maintenance can be less expensive than overhaul or replacement. Just as it is with machinery, the individual needs to continually maintain him or herself when dealing with stress and friction. We do need a regular routine of maintenance in our lives. If we do not take the time away from our work and if we do not make regular "checkup" visits to our doctors, this lack of attention can be extraordinarily expense later.

How will the motives of the ESP affect your responsibilities?

Armed with the knowledge of the list above, the chaplain has the information necessary to more adequately address the needs of the Emergency Services Person. Any mood swings which the ESP encounters can be accessed in light of the "traits" mentioned above. These traits and characteristics are generally standard throughout the emergency services agencies. When the chaplain is aware of the motive behind the action, he/she can begin the process of prevention, maintenance or management when dealing with an employee who is suffering with a personal emotional, physiological, spiritual, or psychological problem.

It is important to communicate to the employee that the very things which make them good at what they do occupationally, will be the things which will become destructive to their family and other relationships. Because of many factors involved in the list of "traits" the employee will find he/she has an enormous load to bear and also has a tremendous responsibility to live up to. This alone will create an inordinate amount of stress, which will manifest itself in the home, at work and in times of recreation and pleasure.

Separating myth from fact about Emergency Services Personnel.

The Community Service Chaplain must enter his/her relationship with Emergency Service Persons with an immediate understanding of the difference between fact and fiction. While it is true that emergency services people are considered a different "breed" of community servant, it is a myth that they are stronger, less prone to emotional outburst or display. Emergency Services Persons suffer from a "disease", which is manifest in one of several forms. The occupational hazard of Police, Fire, Rescue, Emergency Medical Technician, Caregiver and, even Chaplains, is that this type of service infects the caregiver. Metaphorically speaking, it gets into their blood.

In spite of their ability to appear to remain composed and calm during extremely stressful and critical events, they are nonetheless just as subject to all the problems and stress symptoms as any other worker in any other setting. The thing that appears to separate them from others is an inscrutable "code" which belies the truth about the employee. The "code" says, a cop doesn't cry, or a fireman isn't afraid, or an Emergency Medical Technician doesn't mind the sight of blood, the Caregiver can remain above emotions and the list goes on. The truth is, many of these Emergency Service Persons spend a lot of time trying to live up to these images, which results in different types of afflictions or emotional distresses for the above mentioned.

Definitions: Identifying and defining necessary tools for effective Chaplaincy

<u>Perception: Reality but not necessarily truth</u>

By the author's definition, perception is the ability to 'read' or to identify elements of a given situation. For the Community Service Chaplain there are two very important issues to understand about the dynamics of perception. These issues will be discussed at length in the section below, however it will be necessary, first, to understand a very basic principle of crisis intervention.

Perception is Reality.

It cannot be emphasized too strongly the value of understanding the axiom of "Perception is Reality". As simple as it sounds, to understand how the body responds physiological to perceptions around us, is an essential building block to the understanding and the identification of critical issues, and then, the successful intervention and management of these crises.

The argument may be presented that because someone ´perceives´ something, such as a danger, it does not mean that the danger is real or actually exists. While the premise of there statement appears to lie in logic, the overall and comprehensive understanding of the thesis is actually faulty. Most often this statement or premise is made <u>after</u> the fact of the perception, and then, of course, the empirical evidence may support their hypothesis. The flaw in this thinking is that perceptions are not based on established facts or concrete data, but rather on a series of lightening fast thoughts and even, ´feelings´, which take into account the baggage (historical past) of the individual, the context of the situation, to include environmental and political issues, and many other surrounding circumstances and stimuli.

Following are three examples to consider.

Church service interrupted by gunmen.

In 1974 while pastoring a church in East Anglia, just north of London, the author had been preaching a series of eschatological sermons. I made a decision to add a little drama to the final sermon of the series. I obtained the services of three local townsmen to pose themselves as thugs or terrorists. Remember, this is 1974. For purposes of the drama, I obtained three training weapons, which were realistic in appearance and format, but had been mechanically rendered dysfunctional. There was no possibility that the weapons could actually discharge and, additionally, of course, no ammunition was permitted to be used in the "drama". The script had been rehearsed and on this unsuspecting congregation, the men began their actions. In hindsight, the author realizes that *this should never have been done at all*, but the purpose of the account is not to determine the wisdom of the action, but rather, to demonstrate the power of perception. Before continuing with the illustration, the author must remind the reader that in the 1970's, Britain was basically fighting a war of terror. The Irish Republican Army was taking responsibility for bombs which were exploding in department stores and other public areas as well as, what appeared to be indiscriminate car bombings in the northern counties of Ireland and on mainland Britain. Thus the context of the drama being described was not considered in the final outcome of the scenario herein presented by the author.

Upon entering the church the "thugs" disconnected the electrical power and immediately the congregation was in the dark. The men shouted at the congregation to be still and sit down. They used a vocabulary, which church people where not accustomed to hearing, at least in the church environment. Some of the younger male congregation members became belligerent with the "thugs" and were soon put in their places forcibly. The weapons were pointed at the congregation; orders were given to surrender Bibles and songbooks as well as demands of recanting of the faith. At this point, the author himself realized the actual mistake that he had made, because the congregation actually perceived these actions as real. Women and children were crying, men where becoming angry because of the feelings of helplessness and inadequacy to meet the perceived danger.

While, I was aware that there was no true danger, insomuch that the weapons where rendered harmless, no ammunition existed and that the men were not really terrorists, yet within the context of the environment, the immediate perception of danger and other factors which will be described throughout the book, all contributed to the response system of the congregation, going into ´survival´ mode because of the "perception of reality". To the congregation the incident that they were now experiencing was real. Therefore their physiological response system, "fight or fight, was triggered and the essential survival chemicals of the body were now flowing freely and swiftly. The fact of the matter, however, is that, the event, which happened, was real to the perception of the congregation, but it was not truth.

The congregation perceived danger, believed they were in danger and therefore their body responded to this perception. Only after the fear, and anger on the part of some, subsided, did the truth of the matter allow these people to return back to physiological normalcy.

People laughing as one enters a room

A second illustration, however less emotional than the first, is that of two people standing in a classroom. One is telling a joke or funny story to the other. As the storyteller arrives at the point of the "punch line" of the story, a door of the classroom opens. The noise of the opening door distracts, momentarily, both the storyteller and the listener. They turn their gaze upon the door and at the exact moment that an individual walks through the door, the storyteller and listener both burst with laughter. Of course the laughter resulted from the humor of the story. But as the punch line coincided with the person entering the classroom, he now sees and hears both persons looking and laughing at him. The person at the door immediately turns and leaves the room, thinking he must have interrupted a conversation about him or that he is the butt of a coarse joke, which they were telling. Embarrassment was the result of his perception. Of course embarrassment is seen by many as a type of "danger". Upon the perception of this danger, the fight or flight mechanism was employed and the embarrassed individual chose to flee the situation rather than stay and "fight" or confront. As we see from the background, the story was not about the person at all, but rather an innocuous story between friends who actually did not realize how the perception of the other person translated into the reality of fear. The action of the third person was not based on truth but of reality borne out of perception.

The Tax envelope

A third illustration of perception being realty is presented with the following case. Until about the year 2001, the taxation department of the United States Government, known as the Internal Revenue Services or IRS, would send all of its correspondence to tax payers in common, #10 size envelopes. The envelopes, at that time, were brown in color. The contents of the envelope may have been diverse in nature. Change of address, information about change of tax status, overpayment by the taxpayer or an amount due by the taxpayer. All correspondence came in the same brown envelope. Tax time, we understand, can be a very stressful time of the year for many taxpayers. All too often taxpayers are informed by the IRS of insufficient information or assessments, which the taxpayer has sent (or not) to the Internal Revenue Service. Unfortunately along with the assessments came the warning that in the event that the taxes were not remitted in a timely fashion, that the IRS has the authority and power to garnish wages, levy funds from personal bank accounts and/or future earnings. Additionally the employer of the taxpayer would be informed of the delinquency, etc. In fairness to the IRS, this was just a standard letter or warning, indicating what potentially could happen, if the taxpayer did not make arrangements to comply with the paying of taxes found in arrears. However, perception is reality, and many taxpayers would enter into a type of emotional crisis that would have an effect upon them and their families. Eventually the effects that were happening had very little to do with the actual contents of the correspondence that they were receiving, but rather, the existence of the correspondence itself. The potential "danger" was immediately identifiable by the envelope's distinct coloring. This soon became the "trigger" mechanism, which would prompt the fight or flight response in the taxpayer. As the taxpayer, could not fiscally ´fight´ the IRS; he/she would flee from the IRS by ignoring the brown envelopes or procrastinating in the opening of these "bearers of bad news". Did the brown envelopes always bear bad news? Of course not, but perception is reality and not necessarily truth. The greater the negative history that the taxpayer had with the IRS, the more likely his perception will be reinforced.

Grief - The Wound that Time cannot Heal

It has been said, "if a pastor will focus on ministry to the grieving he will never have an empty church".[12] Good grief work is a necessary tool for all Community Service Chaplains. Within the dynamics of grief are found many tools to help the Community Service Chaplain to do intense and powerful ministry. Within this section we find the basic essentials for the Community Service Chaplain to equip him or herself for the necessary understanding of grief ministry.

Time heals all wounds. This is an expression that perhaps all of us have heard. While there is a certain element of truth to this saying in many of life's situations, grief is not one of those situations. The grieving process seems to be such a lengthy and painful process for some individuals and yet others seem to process grief expeditiously, with apparent little pain and a short amount

---

[12] Dr. Robert Crick, International Director Church of God Chaplains Commissions

of time. The truth is, the complexities of the grieving process are subjective to the griever. To begin to understand our grief is to accept the fact that grief never goes away. While the intensity of our grief may lessen, grief is an experience of life that will forever change us.

Even to those of us who have experienced the life changing power of a faith relationship with Jesus Christ, we must also admit that the power of grief is also a force to be understood as a life changing experience.

Most of us, who have a number of years behind us, have experienced grief of one sort or other. It may be the grief of loss, for example a loved one, such as parent or child. Many of our lives have been touched by the grief of a divorce in our immediate or extended family. The acknowledgement of a terminal illness or the loss of reputation due to inappropriate behavior, these are elements of loss that trigger the grieving process. It does not require a lengthy life to have felt the pain of grief.

Grief is a lifelong process. While the pain of loss may diminish in its intensity over time, it never, ever, completely goes away. It is absolutely normal to feel the aftershock of loss for the rest of your life. Martha M. Tousley states that, "Grieving is not a reaction to a single event, like an illness that can be cured and from which you will recover. It's more like a deep wound that eventually heals and closes, but whose terrible scar remains and still can hurt at times."[13] Our life is continually filled with reminders of our loss. This is not really a plague, but rather the reality of the magnificence of our creation. We are creatures of time and therefore, we revisit our life on a

---

[13] *Understanding the Grief Process*, 2005

cyclic basis. We recognize anniversaries, birth dates, holidays and even seasons of the year. As a result of these re-visitations, our mind is prompted to memories of our past. With those memories come sights, smells, touches, tastes and emotions. Because of the wonder of our construction, the grief never completely goes away. With regard to the pain of grief, the intensity of the "re-visits" does lessen over the years. Insomuch that our grief is cyclic; it can be better understood in the sense of a spiral, such as the spring in a ballpoint pen. Imagine that we hold the spring horizontally, and then stretch it a bit. The coils of the spring become distorted. The spirals may become smaller and the oscillations are farther apart. Such is grief. The early grief is long and intense, but as we follow the spiral the coils become small and less intense.

God participates in our grief. It is most difficult to see where God fits into our grief. Grief hurts! We are not accustomed to equating God with pain. It is difficult to comprehend from our understanding of a loving God, just how he allows such deep pain. It is like asking the question, why does God allow babies to die? We never quite get a grip on this. And even if we had a good theological answer, it probably would not be an adequate explanation for the one suffering. God gives comfort — not a painkiller. In comparing our society today to the previous century, Eugene Peterson, author of The Message wrote, "The main difference is not how much people are hurting but how much they expect to be relieved from their hurting."[14] As soon as we feel any kind of discomfort, we look for some

[14] Seven things you need to know about Grief, Focus on the Family, 2005

way to get rid of it. And when someone we love is suffering, we work hard to fix the problem or find a painkiller. But, in truth, God will give us comfort in the midst of the pain. Sometimes there simply is no answer to the pain of grief. It requires the presence of God in the midst of the suffering. It is interesting to see what the writer of Lamentations says about God and grief. Lamentations 3:32: "...though he causes grief, yet he will show compassion."

We grieve differently. We're often surprised to discover that people experience grief in different ways. Jennifer Sands, whose husband died during the terrorist attack on 9/11 said, "Grieving is as individual as a fingerprint."[15] Some of us prefer time by ourselves with an occasional visitor. Others want a steady stream of company and lots of phone calls. In order to help rather than hinder,

---

[15] Ibid.

think about the personality of the person you want to support. It just might make the difference between hurting or healing. A valuable tool is to accept that the person grieving will not grieve the "way" in which we would be most comfortable. Grief, with its many ups and downs, lasts far longer than society in general recognizes. Be patient with grieving people and be patient with yourself as you grieve your loss.

Often a grieving person "violates" the norm that we have set in our life for ourselves and for others. Particularly in our Christian walk we have an expectation of response from people. We expect people to use the accustomed vocabulary, to have learned thoughts about God, etc. Then when a loss occurs, the person doesn't act the way we have come to expect. Because this action is different from what we had come to expect, we now are uncomfortable, because our "pat" answers don't fit the present grief. A great example of this is found in the account of the death of the wife of C.S. Lewis. After Lewis´ wife died from a long struggle with cancer, C.S. Lewis found himself in a deep grieving depression. A close friend who was a clergyman visited Lewis. The well-meaning clergyman touched Lewis on the shoulder and said, "Lewis, your wife is now in the hands of God". With that Lewis replied to the clergyman, almost in anger, "Yes, and that is what bothers me, I have seen what the hands of God have done to her for the past five years".[16]

Comforting the grieving.

Ministering to the grieving person really is an art or talent. There is a tendency to feel normal around those who do not display emotional outbursts during their grieving process,

[16] A Grief Observed. C. S. Lewis, Faber and Faber Ltd., 1961

while, on the other hand, we are discomforted and feel "out of place" when we are attempting to minister to one who is displaying deep distress, anger or acting out. Often our own frustration comes from the fact that we don't have answers for the grieving. We don't feel in control or useful. A terrible tendency of those ministering to the grieving is to try to "get them through it". This serves one purpose, and that is to get the <u>comforter</u> feeling comfortable again. The reality is, "one never gets through it" completely. Allow the process to develop and culminate in healing for the hurting. When comforting the grieving person, remember to talk about their loss. They are grieving because the loss was valuable. They want to talk about it. Often, we are trained to avoid taking about the loss, because we don't know how to handle their crying, or other emotional outbursts. Corrie ten Boom reminds us, "Silence has everything to do with pain."[17]

The worst kind of grief is the grief you're experiencing now. Your grief cannot compare with that of anyone else. The griever must understand that, at this moment, his/her loss is the worst thing that could happen to anyone. Acknowledge that this loss is worthy of grief, and accept that you must endure the very real feelings of sorrow. Whether you are the person grieving or the person extending comfort to the griever, it is important to affirm the reality of the pain. Sometimes, attempting to find something comforting to say, a cliché is uttered, such as "It could have been worse!" There is an intrinsic problem with this

---

[17] Corrie ten Boom in personal interview about Concentration Experience.

thinking.   How could that which did not happen, be worse than that which did happen?

The Traditional five steps of the Grief Cycle.

After Dr. Elisabeth Kübler-Ross, the Dutch doctor wrote her book on Death and Dying, the clinical world used her five-step process as a better understanding of grief. While many other grief "models" have been used, the

Kübler-Ross cycle has found favor as a learning tool for those wishing to understand the dynamics of grief.

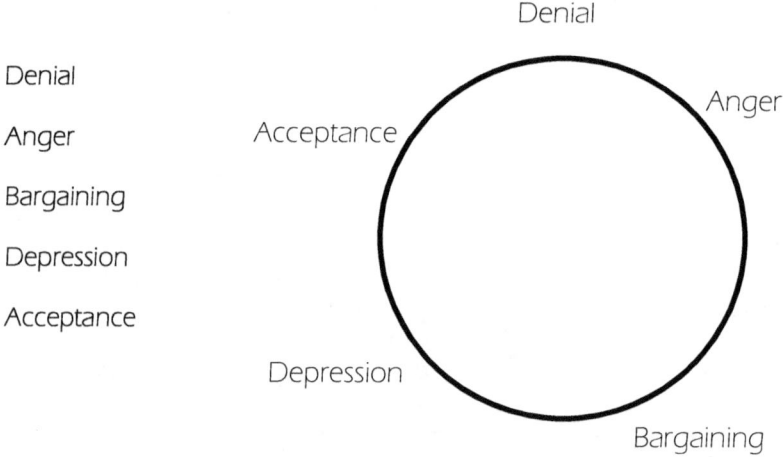

The cycle presented by Dr. Kübler-Ross has five steps or stages to the cycle. 1. Denial, 2. Anger, 3. Bargaining, 4. Depression, and 5. Acceptance.

Denial – Denial is the preliminary or initial phase of grief. It is the point of shock, disbelief and refusal. This stage is also a protective time in the pain of the griever. The emotional shock and disbelief, of course lessens the overwhelming pain that is experienced by the loss.

Anger – Anger is not always an immediate part of the grief cycle, especially with regard go long term illnesses or anticipated losses, but often accompanies a loss that is sudden or unexpected. Often the griever is angry with the person who has died, or fallen ill. Also, the griever often expresses anger at God or God figures, such as pastors or church leaders. With the passing of time, the anger often gets redirected to a more realistic target such as the source of the loss. For example, in the case of an automobile death or severe injury the anger will eventually be directed at the person who caused the accident, even if it is the deceased.

Bargaining – Bargaining is the phase of grief where the griever makes various attempts to compromise or strike a bargain. It is of course a vain attempt to change the inevitable circumstance, but nonetheless is present during the grieving process. For example, a person grieving over the terminal illness of a child will attempt to strike and agreement with God, but declaring their willingness to serve, convert or take on a ministry responsibility if God will heal the child.

The bargaining phase also manifests itself when a person tries (at great expense) many unproven medicines or medical procedures that have a history of futility. The pain of divorce is fertile ground for the bargaining stage. Victims of divorce (in their grief) may go to great lengths to compromise or bargain in order to keep their marriage together. They are often willing to sign any agreement and pay any price in order to demonstrate how much they love the one leaving them.   In the end, this bargaining phase can cost them much more than the divorce. The grief continues.

Depression - The depression stage is the most painful.   Guilt enters into the grief equation.   Suicidal thoughts. Feelings of uselessness and hopelessness are all present in this deep grief. For those who wish to assist the griever, this stage is also the most difficult. Depression is a dynamic most difficult to understand and endure.   The comforter can feel completely incapable of helping the person. Most grievers feel if the depression goes away, that somehow this is a denial of continued care for the loss. All of these guilt complications are very difficult for the caregiver to understand.

Acceptance – There is light at the end of the tunnel. Kübler-Ross contends that as the grief cycle is processed a time of acceptance will arrive. Acceptance is not the end of the grieving, but it allows a tool for the griever, to know that there is hope and a life of happiness in their future. The griever will realize that there has been a terrible loss, which has been extraordinarily painful and confusing, but it is real and I survived it.

During the course of the grief cycle, there may be some relapses. An anniversary date can arrive and the griever may move from <u>Acceptance</u> back to <u>Depression</u>. A financial situation may occur that would not exist if the "husband didn't die." This may cause the griever to revert to anger toward a deceased love one, even after they have processed through the cycle.

Who is predisposed to grief?

This brief section is to inform the chaplain, that no one is exempt from grief. Grief is often identified with loss of life. While this is a correct observation, it is, however, very limited. Grief can result from a victim's perception of loss. Grief is a feeling of "not being able to fix a problem". Grief is a feeling of "believing that life will never be the same again". Grief is a feeling of "My world has changed forever". The chaplain needs to understand that all of these aforementioned feelings are probably true.

Because everyone is predisposed to grief, the chaplain needs to personally reflect upon this issue for him/herself. When the chaplain feels inadequate to assist or help the counselee through the grief cycle, he or she needs understand it is no shame to refer to another who can look at the victim of grief from a new and fresher perspective. This should not be seen as a failing on behalf of the chaplain but rather a credit to his or her professionalism.

What the Chaplain can do in the role of Counselor.

The chaplain will be able to see the situation of the employee victim of grief and identify his or her need for counsel. Initially, the chaplain will be able to assist the employee by implementing a series of responses, which correlate with the circumstances that brought on the grief. By way of example, the chaplain can use the following case study and then the response issues, which follow. This example can be restructured to address the specific circumstances of your employee. Following is another case study from which the chaplain can draw important and valuable information.

Case Study[18]

Six months ago you and your family were returning from church. With the roads slick and wet, you lost control of the car, ran a red light and impacted with another vehicle. As a result of the accident, two of your children (if older, one grown child and a grandchild) along with the couple in the other car were instantly killed. Your companion had serious internal injuries, but survived. The accident left you permanently scarred (with the possibility of extensive plastic surgery), and paralyzed from the waist down. You have had to resign from your church or other position.

As a result of this crisis, respond to the following:

---

[18] A Manual for Community Service Chaplaincy, Jake Popejoy, 1996, pp.50-51

1. How your previous experiences with grief will help or hinder processing your present grief.

2. Your longer-term emotional problems and adjustments at dealing with your grief.

3. How your grief has impacted your concept of God, judgment, grace, the Church and other theological issues.

4. Discuss your grief in terms of your relationship with your companion, your children and others.

5. What resources and persons will you need in dealing with your grief?

6. Will your theology about the protection of God still stand strong, or will you have to altar your theology?

Helpful hints for dealing with grief.

1. Presence, be there; or telephone.

2. Early, frequent, brief contacts.

3. Encourage involvement in plans.

4. Encourage talking about what happened.

5. Encourage talking about the dying or deceased.

6. Include children; comfort children.

7. Discourage chemicals.

8. Don't rush people; give them time to work it through.

9. Allow for strategic withdrawal.

10. Help where there is legitimate dependency.

11. Focus on 'here and now' in the early days.

12. Try to understand grief feelings rather than being annoyed by them.

13. Allow for individual differences.

14. Actualize the sickness or death.

15. Listen.

16. Touch.

Important things to remember when dealing with grief.

Grief, with its many ups and downs, lasts far longer than society in general recognizes.

Be patient with yourself.

Each person's grief is individual

Crying is an acceptable and healthy expression of grief and releases built-up tension for everyone.

Cry freely as you feel the need.

Physical reactions to death may include loss of appetite or overeating, sleeplessness, and sexual difficulties.

You may find that you have very little energy and cannot concentrate.

A balanced diet, rest, and moderate exercise are especially important at this time.

Medication should be taken sparingly and only under the supervision of your physician. Many substances are addictive and can lead to a chemical dependence. In addition, they may stop or delay the necessary grieving process.

Friends and relatives may be uncomfortable around you. They want to ease your pain but do not know how. Take the initiative and help them learn how to be supportive to you. Talk about your loss so they know this is appropriate.

Whenever possible, put off major decisions (changing residence, changing jobs, etc.) for at least a year.

Avoid making hasty decisions about your loved one's belongings.

Do not allow others to take over or to rush you. You can do it little by little whenever you feel ready.

Critical Incident Stress

The understanding of Critical Incident Stress is absolutely necessary to successful ministry in the marketplace. Without the understanding of Critical Incident Stress, the ability to accurately identify crisis stress, and to have a working knowledge of a debriefing, the chaplain will be handicapped in his/her effectiveness in chaplaincy.

Definition of Critical Incident Stress

Critical Incident Stress is identified and defined as stress directly resulting from a trauma or series of traumas. The victim of Critical Incident Stress will most probably suffer a battery of physiological and emotional symptoms. Critical Incident Stress Education is to forewarn and forearm the victim of Critical Incident Stress that when a victim of stress experiences these symptoms that they are in fact normal responses to abnormal circumstances. A definition not to be forgotten is, *"a critical incident is that event that I perceive will forever change the course of my life"*.[19]

Most traumas are subjective to the victim. There are obvious traumas such as loss of life, loss of limb, rape, sudden

---

[19] Jake Popejoy, Community Service Chaplaincy Seminar

blindness and other such tragedy that are objective in their assault on the human body. There are, however, other "traumas" that are definitely subjective to the sufferer. A broken relationship can seem so devastating that one can never recover. Victims can also perceive an automobile accident that involves injury but not loss of limb or life as a critical incident.

Critical Incidents must be interpreted in light of history, context and future potential. Perception truly affects the way that people respond to trauma, but the response that is based on perception only cannot be defined conclusively as a critical incident. If we remember from earlier in this book, "perception is reality, but not necessarily truth". The job of the Chaplain as he or she ministers to a department or agency is to objectively identify what constitutes a critical incident as opposed to a distressing situation which is placing undue stress upon an employee or other individual.

In most cases critical incidents will be obvious as one can identify if an individual's life will be forever changed by the event, e.g., loss of limb, death of a close work partner or family member. However, some incidents, which may not be so objectively categorized, may need be assessed by evaluation of the context in which the event took place. For example, if a woman has a miscarriage of an unborn child. This is of course traumatic, but in and of itself will probably not change the course of the woman's life. However, if she later learns through her gynecologist that she must now have an hysterectomy and can no longer bear children, the miscarriage now becomes a critical incident in a more far-reaching way. Now the definition of crisis is activated. The miscarriage is now *perceived to forever change the course of her life*. So this is now a critical incident that will have to be addressed as such.

The Community Service Chaplain should be informed and educated to know a large number of the symptoms, which accompany Critical Incident Stress.

Following is a brief list of symptoms, which the chaplain needs to commit to memory.

1. Shock

2. Nausea

3. Sleep Disturbances

4. Sexual Dysfunction

5. Hyperventilating

6. Withdrawal

7. Suicidal Thoughts

8. Cynicism

9. Time Distortion

10. Problems with Authority Figures.

A more exhaustive list can be found near the end of the "Manual for Community Service Chaplaincy[20] among the Transparency Templates and identified as "Reactions".

---

[20] A Manual for Community Service Chaplaincy, Jake Popejoy, 1996, pp. 234-235

Adrenaline, epinephrine and other body chemicals

When dealing with a stressed employee and assisting that employee to understand the nature of stress and Critical Incident Stress, it is imperative that the Community Service Chaplain understand, at least to a limited degree, the dynamics of body chemistry. Armed with this knowledge, the chaplain will be able to dispel many fears that are inevitably in the mind of the employee. To understand that the body's chemistry plays a very important part in the way that the employee feels, both physically and emotionally, is a large step toward assisting the individual to recovery and health, insofar as relates to Critical Incident Stress.

Adrenaline is a body chemical that will affect an individual's blood pressure, nervous system, body temperature, digestive system and other physiological responses of the humane body. Epinephrine and Norepinephrine will affect the "feelings" of the body to include emotions such as anger, fear, joy, etc. In laymen's terminology, Norepinephrine is the chemical in the body, which puts the "good" in, feel good. Therefore it is imperative for the Community Service Chaplain to know that the adrenaline and other chemicals, which are produced by the body, are addictive. Therefore, some behavior is difficult to alter because it is a behavioral pattern, which may be part of an addictive process like stress or anger.

Anger is addictive

Anger is addictive. In the early stages of anger the individual has "control" of him/herself, and feels in a position to present an intelligent argument. At some stage in the argument or altercation, the person may feel threatened. The feeling of threat is either physically, emotionally or intellectually. When this sense of "threat" presents itself, the "fight or flight" response is initiated in the body and the chemistry begins. (The fight or flight response will be discussed later.) When the chemistry begins, it is accompanied with the many chemicals of survival, such as adrenaline, dopamine and nor epinephrine. These chemicals give the body an "in charge" feeling, which in and of itself is a good feeling. This is the feeling, which becomes addictive. The great problem with the addiction is that the anger itself rarely stays in control of the individual. Anger crosses a threshold of control into a state of rage. It is in this rage where abuses take place. Abuses can be verbal, psychological, physical and emotional. The person who is caught in this addiction rarely realizes that they are out of control, as they are responding to a perceived threat or danger.

When the anger subsides, the individual(s) declares that they will never again say such cruel things, do such terrible things or belittle the other in such a way. They actually mean exactly what they say. But, just like a person who is addicted to alcohols, drugs or sex, they are drawn back into the addiction when their mind is stimulated to do so. In the case of the "anger addict, it is when they are in another argument and they are confronted with the first sense of perceived danger. The danger can be as simple as, "hey, I think I am going to lose this argument."

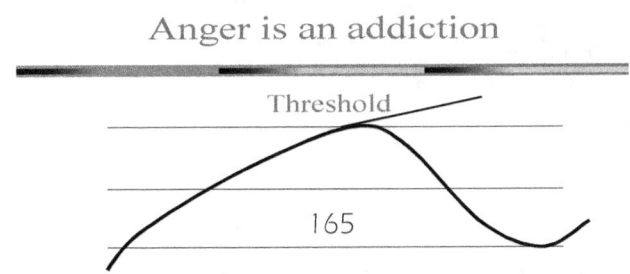

Anger is an addiction

Threshold

165

It behooves the Community Service Chaplain to gain a basic understanding of the body chemistry. It is not necessary that the chaplain to become a "specialist" in this area, but with basic knowledge of body chemistry, the chaplain will begin to understand the dynamics of emotional distresses which affect the employees the chaplain serves.

Fight or Flight Responses

The Fight or Flight responses are basic to all human nature. Most chaplains will have at least an elementary understanding of the Fight or Flight response, which is triggered initially by a sense of peril or threat, after which by the Adrenal Gland.

Adrenal gland   Either of two small, dissimilarly shaped endocrine glands, one located above each kidney, consisting of the cortex, which secretes several steroid hormones, and the medulla, which secretes epinephrine. It is also called suprarenal gland.[21]

Epinephrine. A hormone secreted by the adrenal medulla that is released into the bloodstream in response to physical or mental stress, as from fear or injury. It initiates many bodily responses, including the stimulation of heart action and an increase in blood pressure, metabolic rate, and blood glucose concentration. It is also called adrenaline.[22]

---

[21] The American Heritage® Dictionary of the English Language, Third Edition © 1992 Houghton Mifflin Co. Electronic version lic'd from and portions © 1994 InfoSoft Int'l, Inc.

[22] Ibid.

2. A white to brownish crystalline compound, $C_9H_{13}NO_3$, isolated from the adrenal glands of certain mammals or synthesized and used in medicine as a heart stimulant, vasoconstrictor, and bronchial relaxant.

The implementation of illustrations and case studies where the Fight or Flight response has affected the emotional presence of an individual is necessary to enlighten the afflicted employee. The chaplain and the employee must understand that we are often placed in situations where adrenaline begins its process, but our body is unable to deal with its effects because of the circumstance in which we find ourselves. The fight or flight response to include the activation of adrenaline into the blood system cannot be controlled mentally. As long as there is a perception of danger, the fight or flight response will activate and the adrenal rush will ensue.

Example: An employee has been having some communication difficulty with his boss. The boss calls the employee "into account" in front of other employees. This of course is not a correct or appropriate action by the boss, but it happens nonetheless. The employee suffers embarrassment and frustration. He or she is in a situation where they want to flee or they want to fight, but they can do neither, that is, if they wish to keep their employment. The bodies "juices" are flowing and anger is rising. The employee will begin to respond both emotionally and physiologically in an adverse manner. Thoughts of quitting will be present. This is, of course, the fleeing part of the response. There may be strong "body language" which could indicate resistance or aggression. This will be the fighting part of the "fight or flight" response.

The physiology of the fight or flight response.

Much of this book is devoted to the tools that can help the Community Service Chaplain better minister to those in the church and outside of the traditional church environment. Therefore it is necessary to grasp the physiology of the fight or flight response and commit its mechanics to memory and practice. Following is a brief illustration of the workings of the fight or flight response.

LEO

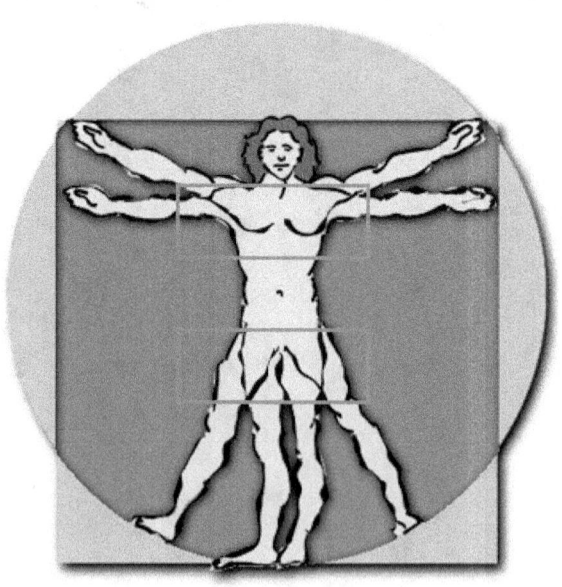

LEO is an acronym for Law Enforcement Officer. In this section of the book we refer to LEO as all Emergency Service Personnel as well as Caregivers.

The Law Enforcement Officer or other emergency responder lives a life of stress like many other people. The problem that LEO has is that his body thinks his lifestyle is normal. As we discuss the dilemma of LEO, the lessons learned will be useful also for the Community Service Chaplain and the pastor. For, in point of fact, they live a lifestyle not unlike LEO.

The flight or fight response initiates with a perceived danger. With LEO this may be a call that he receives on the police radio directing him to a disturbance of some kind. As he is responding to the call, his mind instantly analyzes and confirms that he may be going into a dangerous situation. His mind says, "I don't want to go on this call, but I must, for it is my job". At the instant of perceived danger LEO´s adrenal gland is triggered and the various chemicals, which we discussed earlier, begin to navigate the majority of LEO´s blood to two major muscle groups of the body. (See image above) The blood is directed to the upper torso for the purpose of fighting a perceived danger and to the groin and thigh area for the purpose of fleeing from the perceived danger. It is important to note, that whether LEO actually is in danger or not, does not matter to the adrenal gland. What matters is the "perception" of danger. To the human body responses, "perception is reality".

Often when LEO arrives at the scene to which he has been called, the danger is passed and there is only a report to be taken. But, this doesn't matter to the body, the perception triggered the response and the chemistry was activated driving the blood to the aforementioned muscle groups. It is important to note that when the majority of the blood arrives to its destination, "torso and groin", that there is by default an absence, or rather lack of blood in other areas, such as the brain, vital organs and extremities, i.e., hands and feet. This all means something to us physiologically.

LEO goes back in service after making his report and in a short time receives another call. The same physiological process takes place, because each time LEO responds to a call, his mind says, "I don't want to go to this call, but I must go, because it is my job." Although LEO doesn't actually know if he will be faced with danger and really have to "fight or flee" from this danger, his body still prepares him for the response because of the reality of perception. So again, the blood goes to the two specified muscle groups and leaves the other areas of the body lacking in necessary blood. This goes on day after day, month after month and year after year, until LEO's body believes that the body is normal when it is in a constant state of "fight or flight".

Physiologically, when the body is in this constant state of "fight or flight" it is dangerously deprived of necessary nutrients and the ability to oxygenate the muscles, rid the body of waste and do necessary processing such as digestion and fluid cleansing. Additionally, cognition is greatly hindered because an inadequate amount of blood arrives to the brain. Combine this with the lack of proper circulation and LEO is plagued with a legion of problems. Of course, LEO normally does not realize that his physical problems have anything to do with stress. The fact that his has shortness of breath, back ache, numbness in his hands, feet and face are all things that can paralyze him with fear, yet he is unaware that they are all symptoms of stress as well as stroke and heart attack. Additionally, this kind of stress renders a person prone to poor circulation and of course then the fear of diabetes is present. Compound all of the aforementioned symptoms with fear of the unknown and our LEO is in pretty poor shape.

At this point we must take note that the fight or flight response does not trigger at the point of actual danger, but rather at the perception of danger. <u>Perception is reality but not necessarily truth.</u> Therefore, we see that it isn't the danger that creates the physiological problems mentioned above, but rather the perception of a danger. How is it that this perception invades us so fully? I will call it a "trigger" mechanism. With

LEO it is the daily squelching sound of the police radio. When LEO receives a call from the police dispatcher telling him to respond to a scene, the radio makes a distinct noise indicating that a call is coming to the officer. Herein is the problem. Most of the calls that LEO receives are negative, possibly dangerous. Therefore after weeks and months of receiving such calls, the squelching noise of the police radio is enough to trigger the fight or flight response even before LEO hears the content of the message. So, when LEO receives a message of which is positive in nature, the damage is already done. The fight or flight response has initiated and there is nothing LEO can do about it. Hence, his body believes its existence is normal.

LEO, of course, is not unique. The very same thing can happen to other occupations, but with different "trigger" mechanisms. For sure, with the pastor, the trigger mechanism is the mobile phone, which he or she carries with them almost 24 hours a day. It is not too difficult to see how the mobile phone puts us into the fight or flight response. In the capacity of pastor or chaplain we receive many calls. Of these calls, there are too many which are negative. It can be people leaving the fellowship of the church, complaints about financial accountability in the church, moral failings, children on drugs, bills which need to paid, ad infinitum. Similar to LEO, the pastor or chaplain does not get a steady diet of positive calls. Week after week, month after month, eventually the pastor's body responds to the mobile phone in similar way that LEO responds to the police radio. It does not matter if the caller has something positive to say, the damage is done when the phone rings.

With this knowledge, the Community Service Chaplain is better equipped to assist the parishioners or those to whom he/she ministers outside the traditional church setting. This knowledge helps the chaplain better understand the physiological symptoms that are a result of crisis and stress.

The Dynamics of Fear

This section needs to be addressed and understood well. It is important, however, for the chaplain to note that the dynamics of fear is an advanced issue, which needs to be thought out, and presented from a physiological, psychological and spiritual dimension. One example of the spiritual dimension of fear is to understand that principally, fear is the opposite of faith. Not to be taken to literally, the intention of the statement is to make us aware, that normally we have no fear over any situation in which we feel or sense control.

Therefore, when we are fearful over a spiritual issue, it is normally because we do not feel in control of the situation. Likewise with regard to issues that may not have a "spiritual" implication to them, if we feel in control or more powerful than the situation presenting itself, we do not experience fear. By example, we may have a fear of dogs. Where does the fear actually originate? It comes from the sense of powerlessness with regard to controlling the animal. If we know absolutely, (faith) that the dog is gentle, or that we have control or power over the dog, then our fear diminishes or disappears.

Following is a verbal chart presented by Dr. Roger Solomon regarding the actually dynamic that stimulates Emergency Service Persons during their response to a fearful or dangerous situation. Dr. Solomon identifies six stages of fear during a crisis and puts them in a sequence for the chaplain to both memorize and understand. With this tool, it is most helpful in giving counsel to the survivors of a trauma.

Dynamics of Fear

The Dynamics of a Critical Incident[23]

Here comes Trouble
      -- The situation escalates

Oh my God...this can't be happening
        -- The moment of vulnerability

I've got to do something
      -- We must act to survive

Survival
      -- Focus on the danger

"Here goes"

[23] *Used with permission: Critical Incident Trauma, Roger M. Solomon, Ph.D.*

-- The moment of commitment

Response
    -- We go for it

It is advisable for the Community Service Chaplain an/or pastor to seek out training in Advanced Critical Incident Stress. Suffice it to say at this point, regarding Critical Incident Stress education that....

1. Fear is an automatic emotional response to a perceived danger

2. Fear can be useful

3. Fear is different from Panic

Fear is an automatic emotional response to a perceived danger

Like the adrenaline rush, fear is an automatic response, which the body experience as it perceives the presence of danger. Sometimes fear is experienced during the perception of danger or immediately after the danger has passed. At this point it is important to know that as far as the body and the mind are concerned, perception and reality are one and the same. The body will respond emotionally and physiologically the same to both perceived danger and real danger. Fear follows the same pattern.

Fear can be useful

The idea that fear can be useful is born out of our understanding of survival. We are afraid of being burned, so we learn not to play with fire. We are afraid of drowning so we learn to swim and respect the water. As an employee suffers stress and the emotional baggage, which accompanies a stressful situation, they may find that they have heightened fears about certain situations. By example, missing deadlines, failure to complete tasks or violating company/department policies. All of this can be a sense of frustration to the employee and he/she may believe that they are failures because of fear. The Chaplain can encourage the employee that their fears in stressful circumstances are normal responses to abnormal situations. These are instinctive reflexes, which help us survive threatening, or harmful situations. These situations can be physical, emotional or spiritual.

Fear is different from panic

Very little time will be given to this issue now, as it will be more adequately addressed at later point in the book. The point that needs to be understood at this time is that fear is an emotion that may or may not cause us to do the correct thing at a given time. Panic, however, will normally incapacitate us to the point of doing nothing or surrendering to a situation.

The Four Systems affected by Stress and Fear

The Community Service Chaplain will understand that there are four systems within the human condition that are emphatically affected by stress and fear.

1. The Physical System

2. The Behavioral System

3. The Cognitive System

4. The Emotional System

Each of the four systems mentioned above will have a corresponding chart found near the end of the book.[24]

The chaplain will need to familiarize him or herself with the basic symptoms correlating to each system. Thus the chaplain will be able to identify such symptoms that might be afflicting an employee and if the symptoms exist, be able to educate the employee with regard to identifying and overcoming the emotional and physiological responses to these symptoms.

---

[24] Table 1

Understanding Stress Symptoms

The Community Service Chaplain will be well prepared to give a basic orientation to a stressed employee seeking assistance if he/she has a working knowledge of the information in this book. A few concluding thoughts will serve the chaplain well:

Understand how symptoms materialize - As the Community Service Chaplain understands more about the fight or flight response, it will give a comprehensive understanding of how symptoms materialize. For example, I will use a composition of two police officers that have been my friends for many years. I call the composition of these offices LEO. By giving a basic understanding of the work and responsibilities of LEO, one can begin to see how stress symptoms begin to materialize. This is addressed in detail earlier in this book.

Understand that usual behavior will be altered – The behavior system is one of the four systems of the body, which is affected by stress and crises. Because the physiological changes, which take place, are so intense, it is of no great surprise that behavior is altered when one is under severe stress and crises situations exist. It has been said by Jim Horne[25] "*ONE CRITICAL INCIDENT STRESS EVENT CAN PRODUCE ENOUGH STRESS RESPONSES IN THE BODY TO FOREVER CHANGE THE BRAIN.*"

---

[25] Retired FBI agent, Behavioral Science Division, Quantico, Virginia

It is not unusual to see aberrant behavior in individuals when an actual crisis enters their lives. Such behavior can be identified even when the crisis is perceived and not confirmed as truth. Such is the case with two women who were members of a parish that I pastored a number of years ago. Carol was a young, very pretty Irish lady, approximately 23 years old, long flowing red hair and milky white skin. She came from an ultra conservative Pentecostal background. Carol was very conservative in dress and appearance. She served the church with passion and was dedicated to the mission of Christ. On a given Sunday she came to church dressed in form fitting attire, bedecked and adorned with what might be considered excessive jewelry and cosmetics. The thought of many of the people in the church (to include the author) was that Carol had loosened her morals and perhaps even strayed from the faith. In point of fact, Carol's husband had earlier announced to Carol that he had a mistress and was heavily involved with this woman. As a result of this information, Carol's behavior changed. Perhaps as an act of desperation, perhaps as a way of demonstrating anger to God, but change it did.

Marcia was 32 years old, a platinum blonde, shapely and historically wore form fitting clothing and adornment, quite the opposite of Carol. Marcia had been in the church since childhood and although she attended a very conservative Evangelical church, she was accepted as an active part of the parish. Marcia and her family were known for their musical talent, for commitment to special services, and their willingness to give of their finances. On a particular Sunday, Marcia came to church and she was radically changed. She had no cosmetics, her hair was a bit dowdy and her dress was very modest without the least hint of salaciousness. The thought of many of the conservatives in the church was that Marcia had finally been "saved", or she had a sanctifying experience with the Lord. In point of fact, Marcia was undergoing a similar behavioral change as Carol had experienced. Marcia's husband was faithful and loyal and the problem did not lie with the marriage, but rather, Marcia had learned that an older brother, whom she had not seen for many years, was returning to the local area. This put Marcia in a panic, as this brother had sexually molested Marcia for many years as a teenager. Now Marcia's thoughts were that this terrible time in her life would be exposed to her husband, children and possibly the church. Of course, none of this would happen, but it is indicative of what happens to those who are threatened with a crisis situation. Perception is reality but not necessarily truth.

The two true scenarios mentioned above, happened to these women who had the possibility of a support system, the church. When such behavior occurs in the market place and there is no one like a chaplain or pastor to understand that behavioral changes are normal symptoms in time of crises, the victim of such crisis can think that they are actually having psychological problems rather than physiological problems.

Understand that behavioral changes are not necessarily character changes. – Often a Community Service Chaplain can identify behavior changes by having an intimate knowledge of the character of those to whom he/she ministers. This begs the question of relationships and time involved with these relationships. The point I wish to draw is that because we see an individual or individuals acting or behaving in a socially non-acceptable manner, it does not mean that the character is faulty. To have an intimate understanding of the individual(s) will allow us to assess the character. Then, when we see aberrant behavior (for the individual), we have a signal or signals that tell us that the individual is suffering from a crisis or stress related situation.

Before leaving the subject of Fear, it will be necessary to provide another tool for the Community Service Chaplain with regard to the power of fear. Fear, as mentioned early, can be seen as the opposite of faith. Fear has the ability to prohibit people from becoming intimate with each other. The intended meaning of intimacy is not in the sexual sense exclusively, but rather intimacy, which allows interpersonal relationship and interaction. I intend an intimacy that gives ability to know the deep needs and motivations of another. Patricia Sheehan, a former combat nurse in Vietnam, proffers the thesis that there are five such fears that inhibit good interpersonal relationships. Sheehan identifies the following fears.

1. Fear of Merger

2. Fear of Abandonment,

3. Fear of Exposure

4. Fear of Attack

5. Fear of your own destructive impulse

The first of the five fears presented by Sheehan is the <u>Fear of Merger</u>. This fear is the fear of losing one's own identity or the fear of being out of control of a given situation. It is a basic refusal of give and take in a given relationship, whether the relationship is a marriage, a job, church or other significant position. A very basic illustration of the fear of merger, within western society, is the more contemporary phenomenon of women keeping their maiden names upon marriage. Historically, in western culture, the wife took the name of the husband. While there is, of course, nothing intrinsically wrong with keeping one's maiden name, it can be construed as part of the fear of merger that does not allow people to become complete interwoven with each other.

The second of the five fears is the <u>Fear of Abandonment</u>. This fear is the fear of loving and then losing the one(s) that one loves. This fear is rooted in diverse thinking and experiences. In the law enforcement and fire brigade services, the fear of losing ones spouse through death can be a present and daily fear. The idea of losing the loved one through tragic circumstances can place a terrible weight upon intimate relationships. Additionally, the Emergency Services are statistically rife with divorce and affairs. Therefore this brings to the spouses another type of fear of abandonment.

The third of the five fears is the <u>Fear of Exposure</u>. This fear is terrible and awesome. It is a fear that pervades every aspect of relationships and is present in every conversation. This is the 'shame factor'. This is the possibility of the exposure of both the <u>known</u> and the <u>unknown</u> character flaws. These can include homosexuality, deviations and perversions. This is the fear that previous behavior and relationships will be exposed to one which you love.

The fourth fear of intimacy is the <u>Fear of Attack</u>. This is the fear of being hurt, both physically and emotionally. This hurt or attack comes from demeaning criticisms, abusive situations and public embarrassments. This fear can be considered proactive insomuch that when one perceives that they are going to be hurt; there is a tendency to hurt the hurter first. Of course the obvious problem with this is the formulation of a protracted power struggle, which cannot be healthy for any relationship.

The fifth fear of intimacy presented by Sheehan is the <u>Fear of Destructive Impulses</u>. This is the fear of our own ability to hurt our self or to hurt others. This can relate both to physical and emotional. It often involves money issues, moral issues, sex, drugs and other issues such as co-dependency. People who have historically suffered from low self-esteem or have been sexually violated by family members or authority figures appear to be predisposed to this fear of destructive impulses.[26]

---

[26] R. A. Steffenhagen, and Jeff D. Burns, *The Social Dynamics of Self-Esteem: Theory to Therapy* (New York: Praeger, 1987), 104.

The Chaplain and Stress Management.

Stress management can be a very exciting topic because of its importance, but generally it is often seen to be exceedingly boring. The reason for the boredom is that the subject has saturated our society, insomuch that very few people have ever really learned to manage stress. The actually idea of talking about it, or learning something new, seems to be an exercise in futility or at the very least merely academic. The Community Service Chaplain will assist the employee whom he/she serves by helping them understand the major increments of stress, what is the significance of each increment, and how the symptoms might materialize within each increment.

The Three Increments of Stress:

The Community Service Chaplain must recognize that stressors and the existence of stress itself can be identified in increments. There is a distinct difference between the intensity of stress and the incremental processes of stress. Often a stress symptom is in response to a single stressful incident, such as an extremely painful toothache. We can see that this stress has an effect on the four systems of the body, which are affected by stress. Behavior is changed, emotions are at a peak, the physical implications are obvious and cognition is affected because of one's preoccupation with this terrible pain. But, thankfully, this stressor will pass hopefully sooner than later.

Following is an example of acute stress condition or syndrome.

• Acute Stress Condition – Acute Stress Condition or Syndrome is a singular act or stressor that brings about a set of conditions. The conditions will obviously be determined by the history of the person that experiences the stressor. Symptoms of Acute Stress will develop rather quickly. For example, a rookie firefighter responds to his first fire. Unfortunately there is a victim of the fire who has been terribly burned. As a result of the sights, sounds and smells, the firefighter may immediately demonstrate symptoms of this crisis that he is witnessing. Vomiting may ensue, a sense of panic and fear, (for he may have to find another victim) and even feelings of shame. These responses happen rather quickly and somewhat aggressively.

- Delayed Stress Condition - In laymen's terms, delayed stress condition or syndrome is a series of stressors gathered during the course of several traumatic events. Additionally, it can be a serious trauma or critical incident which requires the victim of the crisis or trauma to continue acting in a professional manner until a "break" is found, which then allows the victim to experience symptoms of stress. A prime example of such delayed stress is found in a funeral. For example, Dad dies a sudden death such as heart attack or stroke. This is terrible and grievous, but many things have to be done. Funeral arrangements have to be made, hotels, food, service, liturgy, etc. The process is extended because the family wishes to wait on relations who are coming from afar. Finally, the funeral is past, the family goes home, and you are left alone. It is common during this time for the grieving person to manifest multiple symptoms of the stress and trauma, which they have just been through. They will cry, be angry, sleepless, experience loss of appetite and have intense feelings of being overwhelmed.

They may have intrusive images or voices of the deceased. All of this is normal as relates to Delayed Stress Syndrome.

According to Widdison and Salisbury a significant aspect of the problems attributed to Delayed Stress Syndrome is the result of grief-related reactions to significant losses that were repressed while in the service because American culture, coupled with military training, did not facilitate the expression of such emotions. It was not until the individual separated from the service and returned home that defense mechanisms could relax, allowing the emergence of the repressed grief.[27]

---

[27] Widdison, H. A., and Salisbury, H. G. (1990). "The delayed stress syndrome: A pathological delayed grief reaction?" *Omega*, 20(4), 295.

- Cumulative Stress Condition – The effects of Cumulative Stress Condition or Syndrome are carried over a much longer period of time. In fact the stressors can be "stored" in the life of the individual for years. If an Emergency Service Person perceives that they have to withhold or conceal their emotions because of the type of job that they have, the likelihood of Cumulative Stress Condition increases proportionately. The vocabulary, which is "learned" on the job, can be a devastating element that contributes to this Cumulative Stress Condition. For example, in jobs heretofore perceived to be male dominated such as Police and Fire, the officer suffering from stress has heard it said that "real men" don't cry. Expressions like, if you "can't take it", get out of the job. Or if "it's too hot", get out of the kitchen, all contribute to a wrong headedness with regard to stress and the management of stress.

Some Emergency Service Persons have gone through many years of their careers with having experienced strong or compelling symptoms of stress. As a result of this, there is a feeling of invincibility or immunity to stress. This becomes a huge problem when a tiny stressor sends the individual in an emotional tailspin. They are puzzled, worried and confused about what brought about this terrible emotional upheaval. The fact of the matter is that the Emergency Service Person was accumulating the stressors over a period of years and the tiny stressor, which triggered the emotional devastation, was actually the "straw, which broke the camel's back". A point in case is a female police officer that was one of the first females to enter the police department in her small community of 30,000 people. As mentioned earlier in the paper, stress and crisis must be evaluated in light of the individual's history and context. This woman had a previous marriage to a minister who had been physically and emotionally abusive to her. She endured the marriage as long as she could and left the marriage feeling spiritually destitute and ashamed. She watched the perpetrator of her abuse, (ex-husband) go unpunished by the law and the ecclesiastical authorities. In the process of this marriage and subsequent divorce she learned that she was unable to have children. In the midst of all of this adversity, she remained strong and "in control". The psychology of her situation drove her to apply as a police officer. She was accepted and passed the academy and received her first assignment. She received ridicule from her colleagues, principally because she was a woman.

Officers insinuated that she could not do the job effectively and expressions of doubt about her reliability in a crisis were always in the air. She had two experiences with sexual harassment in the workplace and settled both of these situations without going to court. Several years passed and she continued to do her job in the midst of past and present stressors. On her way to work one Monday morning, she broke a fingernail while changing gears during the drive. This small, relatively insignificant stressor was the "straw that broke the camel's back". Upon arriving at work, she was angry, shouting even to the point of hysterical screams. She entered the building slamming a door, which caused glass to break and went into the changing room where she locked herself in and would allow no one to enter or exit. Fortunately she was a close friend of the department chaplain. He was called to the police department and there defused this situation. Of course her first comment was, "why am I doing this because of a broken fingernail"? The answer, when seen objectively, is simple. It was a near classic case of Cumulative Stress Condition.

Pre-Critical Incident Education

Assimilation and Categorization

The principles of Assimilation and Categorization are extremely important in helping an employee or counselee to understand something about the psychological baggage, which they are carrying. This principle may seem overly simplified, yet the Community Service Chaplain will find it very useful, both in his or her personal life and as they counsel and minister in the workplace.

Merriam – Webster renders the definition of assimilation as *"the process of receiving new facts or of responding to new situations in conformity with what is already available to consciousness"*.

Assimilation is absolutely vital in understanding the affects of stress upon our lives. As intelligent adults we already have an academic understanding of many things. Most of what we know however is assimilated into our life rather than researched, proven and systematically integrated into our life at appropriate times. To give example of this I present the following axiom.

Assimilation - *If it has four legs and a tail and stands in a pasture, it must be a cow. Therefore, if I have a headache, I must have a brain tumor.*

The italicized statements above are not meant to be facetious or absurd, but rather to suggest a thought process that all too often occurs in the thinking of those who are undergoing emotional stress and problems.

<u>Assimilation can be seen in the following example.</u>

The father of a very young child places the child on his knee to read the child a book. As the father leafs through the book, he turns to a picture of a cow. The father asks junior if he knows what this is. The boy may never have seen a cow before and does not know what a cow is. The father tells the child that the picture is of a cow, and then tells the child what sound a cow makes - "moo". He asks the child again and the child repeats what Dad has told him the child attempts the mooing sound. As the father turns the page, he views a horse. He asks the child if he knows what this animal is and the child responds by saying it is a cow and thus makes a mooing sound. The father corrects the child and says, while it has four legs, a head, a tail and stands in the pasture, as does a cow, it is in fact a horse and not a cow. The father instructs the child in the sound of a horse - "winnie or neigh". As the father proceeds through the book, he sees a donkey... and as one can imagine, the child is really confused.

This is what adults do as well. Adults work out of their learned knowledge. Therefore, if a man or woman has been told that severe headaches are a symptom of a brain tumor or an aneurysm, they will most likely respond emotionally and their body will respond physiologically to what they believe is the truth. The emotional and physical responses will continue until the person has learned how to Categorize.

Categorization - *The ability to take the generalities of a subject, that is, person, place, thing, or concept, and recognize the specifics, in order to identify an item in consideration.*

To understand the italicized statement above, it is necessary to go back to the illustration of the father and the child reading the book. Once the child learns to look for detail and gains an eye for animals and learns the distinctives of each, he is then using the tool of categorization. Even the eye of the child will be able to distinguish between the horse and a donkey, or a goat and a ram.

Therefore, it may be important for an employee who is depressed because of chronic headaches and is afraid to go to the doctor, to understand that headaches may be stress related because of constricted blood flow due to the fight or flight responses, etc. Or a person, who has daily tightness in the chest and difficulty breathing, need not unduly believe they are having a heart attack, when this too could be the onset of a panic attack or something much simpler such as the symptoms of an extremely stressful situation, which has produced anxiety symptoms.

Important - The Community Service Chaplain must always encourage an employee to seek medical advice and assistance in the event of physical symptoms. While stress will produce many symptoms that correspond to heart attack, stroke and other serious illnesses, it is vital to learn if the employee indeed is suffering from a physical malady.

Post Traumatic Stress Disorder

The average person recovers nicely from Critical Incident Stress. However, if not dealt with adequately, it can result in Post Traumatic Stress Disorder.

Post Traumatic Stress Disorder also known as PTSD is a pathological disorder.

Post-Traumatic Stress Disorder (PTSD) is a delayed but persistent condition characterized by depression, guilt, and grief, as well as a re-experiencing of a trauma in the form of flashbacks or nightmares and intense anger, anxiety, and emotional detachment. It is the response to being exposed to a traumatic and unusual event.[28]

Merriam-Webster defines pathology as 2: *something abnormal: a: the structural and functional deviations from the normal that constitute disease or characterize a particular disease b: deviation from propriety or from an assumed normal state of something nonliving or nonmaterial.*

Based on this definition, we see that when stress has accumulated so strongly and intensely, a physiological change takes place in the life of the individual suffering from such pathology. Hence, PTSD is the on the extreme edge of what we commonly call stress. The person suffering from PTSD is

---

[28] Alicia Skinner Cook, and Daniel S. Dworkin, *Helping the Bereaved: Therapeutic Interventions for Children, Adolescents, and Adults* (New York: Basic Books, 1992), 25.

sick. They generally act out and deviate from normal social behavior. Social graces are no longer important nor do they exist in any recognizable form any longer for this person in crisis. In fact the action can be so devastating that the individual takes the lives of others or his/her own life. We should note at this point that there are two interesting phenomenon to observe.

First. During the Vietnam War and shortly thereafter, Vietnam veterans received certain preferential treatment with regard to government jobs. The United States Postal Service was inundated with returning veterans. Many of these veterans had spent months, even years in combat. They returned to the USA without counseling and without an awareness of the damage that had been done psychologically to their emotions and spirit. Many of these postal employees struggled with PTSD and lost the battle. Some would enter their workplace, angry at authority, at themselves and at life in general. Eventually, a number of these employees would ultimately kill many of their colleagues and finally themselves.

Second, it is important note an interesting statistic about death with regard to the Vietnam veteran. During the 10 years of America's involvement in Vietnam, there were more than 58,000 men who died in combat action. During the immediate 10 years following America's withdrawal from Vietnam, 117,500 Vietnam veterans took their own life. Interestingly, this ratio also appears to hold true in the Law Enforcement community. Generally, for every officer who loses his/her life in the line of duty in any given year, twice that number take their own life during that same year.

The Chronology of the Pathology is as follows:

1. The event

2. Physical symptoms

3. Emotional symptoms

4. Cognitive dysfunction

5. Hyper arousal in all categories

6. Fear of repetition

7. Recurrence of event – flashbacks, dreams and intrusive images.

8. Symptoms must last longer than 30 days to be diagnosed

Statistics from United States Veterans Affairs Department

40% of people with physical trauma will get PTSD

50% of sexual assault victims will get PTSD

60% of incest victims will get PTSD with the majority attempting suicide

70% of people who witness torture will get PTSD

90% of torture victims get PTSD

What Is Crisis Counseling?

Crisis counseling is not intended as long term and is often understood to be no more than 1 to 3 months. The focus is on a single, (such as a critical incident) or recurring problems that are so overwhelming as to be traumatic. If a trauma or crisis is not resolved in a healthy manner, such as a Critical Incident Stress Debriefing then the experience can lead to more lasting problems such as depression or Post Traumatic Stress Disorder.

The Community Service Chaplain must be aware that crisis counseling is not a substitute for individuals who need long term professional care such as psychotherapy or other long term psychiatric care. The chaplaincy and crisis counseling may involve outreach, on scene support, work with in a community and is not limited to office appointments.

There are many descriptions and a great deal written about crisis intervention and crisis counseling. Regardless of the theory and author, there are universal "elements" in the process by which a crisis counselor can help people face and move past distressing and traumatic events in their lives.

Following is a list of 7 Elements of Crisis Intervention and a brief synopsis of each.

Education. There is a natural ability within most people to recover from a crisis provided they have the support, guidance and resources they need. The very heart of crisis intervention is to face the impact of a crisis and where possible to re-empower the traumatized. In most cases, a crisis involves normal reactions and symptoms, which are not always understandable, but are consistent to an abnormal situation.

Effective crisis counseling provides information; activities and structure that will help one recover and move past the crisis. More importantly, crisis counseling will insure that one does not prolong a crisis and it will help insure one does not create more problems for one's life and the lives of others. Confrontation through information and discussion may be an important part of crisis intervention. Jay Adams, a Presbyterian minister and author, says that this type of confrontation with the crisis requires a nouthetic approach to counseling. It is a matter of talking about the event, accepting the facts of the trauma and finding a healthy process to heal from the crisis.

Observation and awareness. A crisis in our life, but not necessarily a critical incident, can be the result of low self-awareness or not recognizing the impact our behavior has on others as well as the impact it has on our self. Increasing your awareness can lead to choices that promote recovery and wellness. You can't help yourself if you cannot see the problem and how you may be contributing to the crisis. In some cases, family dynamics and communication problems within families can prolong a crisis. This is especially noticeable in marital situation where there has been a long-term struggle for power.

Understanding our problems. It is the fundamental intention of all people to do the best they can with the resources and abilities they have during a crisis. During any crisis, it is important to recognize or discover our true and deepest intention. While it may not be possible at the moment of a crisis or trauma one must, nevertheless keep his/her intentions in mind no matter how unskillfully one may act. While our intent is usually to make life better, our behavior can be misguided, misunderstood and less effective than we would hope. Self-understanding as well as understanding how others may keep us "stuck" are important keys to recovering from a crisis.

Creating necessary structure. The most important aspect of crisis intervention and counseling is to provide a social "container" for our experience that will allow us to express, explore, examine and become active in ways that help insure the crisis is not prolonged. An understandable structure for everyday living is vitally important for the management and coping with stress and its symptoms. For each of us, there are necessary activities and routines in our life during times of distress that provide comfort and support. These **do not** include alcohol, medications or other drugs. Medications should only be used to prevent a physical or psychological breakdown.

When it is necessary for medication to become a part of the coping mechanisms of stress management the understanding of the purpose, duration, frequency and potential impacts of medications must be defined in order to make informed decisions.

Challenging irrational beliefs and unrealistic expectations. Few people, during times of crisis, have the necessary skills to understand, let alone fully examine what they are thinking during or after a trauma. Therefore they cannot fully comprehend what they expect from themselves and from others. One's thoughts, especially the ones we don't know how to articulate, contribute a great deal to how we feel and what we do next in response to our feelings.

Breaking vicious cycles of behavior.

Many crises are the result of vicious cycles or addictions. For example, drug and alcohol use cannot only destroy our life, but it will confuse how we actually feel about our self, others and the world around us. One cannot know how they feel and what they truly want if chemicals, medications, alcohol and other drugs modify their feelings.

A painful crisis can lead a person to avoid and escape how they feel. Unhealthy escape and avoidance of emotional pain and distress may involve the use of medication, drugs, alcohol, and sex; thrill seeking, parties and/or working excessively. Taking the role of a "victim" can cause others to rescue a person in crisis. Prolonging the crisis by refusal to deal with a crisis can create supportive relationships. When a person becomes dependent on others and "escapes" to feel better, a vicious cycle can develop.

Vicious cycles start with behaviors that are intended to avoid or escape emotional pain, but ultimately these avoidance and escape behaviors create more problems or the same problem we are trying to avoid. The behaviors found in a vicious cycle can actually prolong a crisis.

Create temporary dependencies. During a crisis, it is often helpful to form brief relationships with others in order to gain support. Depending upon the type of crisis, the process of unhealthy triangles can develop and become a counterproductive part of the crisis counseling process. The Community Service Chaplain is therefore advised to educate him/herself with regard to such triangles and understand the rudimentary basics of psychology.

Crisis counseling and intervention are very helpful and necessary. A healthy dependency is usually temporary and will generally lead to increasing independency. Unhealthy dependencies are long term and create increasing dependency rather than independency.

Facing fear and emotional pain. A crisis is usually a time of fear and/or sadness. How we respond is important. There is a "monster" in the world for every person who "runs" in response to their fear or sadness. In his account of his most traumatic and stressful time in a Nazi concentration camp, Viktor Frankl asserts that such pain, stress and depression can tend to di-dignify a person. Frankl's struggle was to retain self respect and thereby strip the emotional pain that he was experiencing of its power of his future. Frankl would note, "If the man in the concentration camp did not struggle against this [loss of human values] in a last effort to save his self-respect, he lost the feeling of being an individual, a being with a mind, with inner freedom and personal values. He thought of himself then as only a part of an enormous mass of people; his existence descended to the level of animal life." As Frankl so eloquently testifies, the right to produce with pride, purpose, and dignity is a fundamental human need. [29]

When we face the darkness in our life, and we are not destroyed by our fears, or sadness, we eventually discover there are no monsters. We discover that we can survive. In time we discover that our pain will fade. Facing emotional pain is the healthiest response. This does not mean we should make our self-miserable. But we should not spend or rather "waste" a great deal of energy and become involved in activities that help us avoid how we feel and what we think. When people suffer, it

[29] *Man's Search for Meaning*, psychiatrist Viktor Frankl (1963), page 79

is important to help them feel less alone in the world. It is important to help people in crisis solve the problems in their life. People in emotional pain need to be empowered and supported.

Critical Incident Stress Debriefing – A subtle aspect of Crisis Counseling.

Critical Incident Stress Debriefing is a phenomenon of the 1980. The author's experience with this counseling dynamic came from my work and involvement with the Federal Bureau of Investigation in Quantico, Virginia. In the emergency services and especially law enforcement community it is quite difficult to convince such macho oriented men and women that they need counseling. The very idea of "counseling" smacked of a lack of control or even a mental problem. These strong willed men and women would often have none of that. Somehow, to these employees a <u>debriefing</u> sounded more "job" oriented and less like a counseling session. The Critical Incident Stress Debriefing became a premier form of counseling among the FBI and other federal agencies. Consequently, local agencies adopted the process because of its acceptance at the federal level.

Emergency Service Persons and workers in emergency medical services daily exposed to stresses not normally encountered by the lay public. While we share the happiness of victims and families who get better because of their efforts, we also share in the frustration and sorrow of those who suffer because of traumas and crises, which are experienced by these servants of the community.

Part of the job is maintaining a critical balance between empathy and a certain desensitization that allows the Emergency Service Persons to effectively perform their jobs. Sometimes, however, situations or crises occur that have them experience emotions that are overpowering and can actually interfere with one's ability to function.

Situations, such as these, are known as "Critical Incidents". They are those events that cause one to believe that their life will forever be changed by this trauma or crisis.

It is easy to understand that a terrorist bombing and its aftermath of destruction would easily qualify as critical incidents, but there are other, more common events that are just as devastating. These include the suicide of a co-worker, the sudden death of a child, treating a victim of child abuse or treating a friend who is critically injured in an accident. Sometimes critical incidents are less well defined; in laymen's terms, a critical incident is any incident that the individual worker feels is critical to them.

Emergency Service Person and the Community Service Chaplains who are exposed to the stress created by critical incidents are proven to be much more prone to developing professional burnout. They may develop symptoms of posttraumatic stress disorder: difficulty sleeping, depression, recurrent nightmares, "flashbacks", and a general inability to continued functioning effectively in their chosen occupations.

The result of this is that every year we lose some of the best trained and most experienced emergency workers to the effects of chronic critical incident stress.

In recent years the emergency medical services, in conjunction with mental health professionals developed a program known as Critical Incident Stress Management.

The Jeffrey T. Mitchell Model of Critical Incident Stress Debriefing[30]

When a critical incident occurs, a debriefing should take place within 24 to 72 hours of the incident. During the debriefing, the individuals involved in the critical incident meet with a team of peer counselors and mental health professionals to discuss the incident and begin processing and working through it.

---

[30] Critical Incident Stress Debriefing: Cisd : An Operations Manual for the Prevention of Traumatic Stress Among Emergency and Disaster Workers

According to Mitchell a debriefing is held in 7 phases. Following is a short outline of Dr. Jeffrey T. Mitchell's model of Critical Incident Stress Debriefing.

Introduction: Individuals are assured that everything discussed during the debriefing will be kept confidential. Nothing said in the debriefing will affect their job in any way. Additionally, the person(s) being debriefed are asked if there is anyone present that they do not wish to be in the debriefing. It is, of course, necessary that the members of the debriefing team have advanced knowledge and training regarding this question. Therefore, if the person being debriefed indicates that they would prefer that a particular member not be present, it is incumbent upon that member to immediately dismiss him or herself.

Facts: Individuals get to go over actual details of the critical incident. This may require a little encouragement, in some cases, as they have probably told their story many times previous to the debriefing. Some facilitators advise that if a person does not wish to speak or express himself or herself it is not necessary. However, it is often proven that when more than one person is being debriefed that after one person gives an account of the facts, that it motivates others to do so by their own choice.

Thought: (Authors Note) In recent years the Thought Phase has been removed from Mitchell's model by some debriefers. I am presenting it here for the Community Service Chaplains, as I have found it a most powerful part of the debriefing, especially when ministering to Emergency Service Persons.

Some mental health professionals attempt to integrate the idea of feelings into this phase and also the following phase, but the author has experientially found the talk of feelings to be unproductive, as feelings are too difficult for a traumatize person to articulate, but the ability to articulate thoughts remain rather lucid in the mind of the person in crisis.

Reactions: The group, specifically those having experienced the traumatic event, discuss their reactions about what happened. This is a time of expected emotions and emotional responses.

Symptoms: Those being debriefed are encouraged to discuss any mental, physical or emotional symptoms they experienced during the incident and are, if any, experiencing after the incident. This is a time for the facilitators to reinforce the emotional strength of those being debriefed. Giving assurance that symptoms that result from the incident are generally normal responses to an abnormal event or situation often does this.

Teaching: The debriefers help give meaning to their feelings and the symptoms that the members have described. They help them to see that their reactions are normal. Additionally, they give some basic instruction on diet and exercise. This is, however, not a time to deliver a stress management class.

Re-entry: The debriefers evaluate information discussed in the meeting and offer suggestions as to how the participants can deal with the stresses and actually help them form a plan for returning to their job. If needed, plans are made for follow-up activities or treatments. The debriefers assure those being debriefed that they are available for contact and interaction if needed.

Follow-ups can be held weeks or months later if needed to address any unresolved issues A debriefing should include everyone involved in the incident; nurses, police, Emergency Service Workers, fire and rescue personnel. In some case it may even be appropriate to include spouses, as they are the ones who are so frequently exposed to the after effects of critical incident stress.

Mitchell also teaches another specialized version of Critical Incident Stress Debriefing which is known as "Defusing". Defusing is an abbreviated, earlier form of Critical Incident Stress Management that usually involves only the people who were the most directly involved in the incident. A defusing normally takes place at or near the incident and is done with the permission of the chain of command. It usually lasts only fifteen to twenty minutes and sets the stage for later full debriefings. In the Oklahoma City bombing, as emergency workers finished their shifts, they attended defusings and later debriefings.

Critical Incident Stress Management works by helping individuals vent their reactions rapidly. This aids in the more rapid processing and assimilation of the experiences and emotions that occurred in response to the critical incident. When Critical Incident Stress Management is properly utilized it drastically reduces the subsequent development of symptoms of posttraumatic stress and professional burnout.

A graphic of the Mitchell model can be found at the end of the book. The author has made an alteration to the model in order to accommodate the Emergency Service Persons that tend to have a different dynamic when involved in a debriefing. As the reader will see, the second phase or stage is altered in order to be able to educate the Emergency

Service Person as to the reasons why they should participate in a critical incident stress debriefing.[31]

The Bohl Law Enforcement Model[32]

Dr. Nancy K. Bohl is a leader among crisis counselors. She works predominantly with Law Enforcement communities, but her Debriefing Model of course can be used cross-career. Following is a brief outline that describes her debriefing model.

The debriefing technique, which Bohl uses with police officers, derived originally from the pioneering work

---

[31] Table 2

[32] Martin I. Kurke and Ellen M. Scrivner, eds., *Police Psychology into the 21st Century* (Hillsdale, NJ: Lawrence Erlbaum Associates, 1995) 174.

of Jeffrey T. Mitchell. Although Mitchell's model provided a basis, Bohl found, after continued work with police officers over the years, that Mitchell's approach--which was developed to treat firefighters and other disaster workers-- needed to be modified in a number of significant ways when the individuals being treated were police officers.

Bohl insists that a Critical Incident Stress Debriefing should be carried out within three days and the earlier the better.   Bohl also insists that the debriefing should be understood by the police officer(s) to be mandatory. The author disagrees with this last statement, as it has been his experience that to make a debriefing mandatory takes away the control of the situation from the officer. *Stress is, in point of fact, caused by being out of control of any given*

situation. Therefore the idea of a mandatory debriefing is counter productive to the purpose of the debriefing.

As opposed to Dr. Mitchell's model, Bohl implements 9 steps or phases to the debriefing process. Each phase is briefly described below and should be a memorized tool for the Community Service Chaplain.

Phase 1. The first phase is **the introduction**, the purpose of which is to make clear to participants the nature of the process and who will be involved. Participants are told not only what the debriefing involves but also what it does not involve. Specifically, they are told that the purpose of the debriefing is to aid in recovery, and they are assured that information obtained during the debriefing will be confidential. Unlike Mitchell, Dr. Bohl does not take pains to tell the person(s) being debriefed that they do not have to speak. She finds this caution unnecessary, as her findings are that less than 5% of those being debriefed actually elect to be silent.

Phase 2. In Bohl's model, the second phase is a **fact phase**, during which participants tell what happened during the incident. The facilitator asks questions like the following: Where were you during the incident? Tell me about the experience. What was your role?

Phase 3. In Bohl's model as in Mitchell's, Phase 3, the **thought phase**, is one in which participants describe their thoughts during the stressful event. This phase is like the thought phase employed by Mitchell, except that participants are asked about all of their thoughts and not necessarily what occurred to them first, as in Mitchell's model. A further difference has to do with the previously mentioned distinction that Mitchell attempts to make between cognitive and emotional domains.

Phase 4. In Bohl´s model, phase 4 is the **feelings or reaction** phase, the purpose of which is to allow participants to express the emotions associated with the critical incident. At this time, the facilitator goes back to the factual statements made earlier by participants about their actions during the critical event. They are asked about what their feelings were while they were carrying out the actions they described earlier. For example, a participant might be asked: What did you feel when you realized that you had shot the suspect? What did you feel when you thought your partner had been shot? **Authors note:** (I wish to note at this point, that if a Community Service Chaplain uses Bohl´s model as opposed to Mitchell's, that Phase four can be very volatile as her model requires that one ask for "feelings" rather than thoughts. This is awkward at best and probably dangerous. I have found that it is not possible for someone to be able to articulate feelings that they are experiencing for the first time, such as the crisis in question. The result of asking these questions about feels can be anger and even acting out toward the facilitator.)

What is helpful for participants is not the mere expression of emotions but rather the opportunity to validate feelings. Often, it is a revelation to discover that peers had similar feelings.

Sometimes, police officers that were eager to speak during the fact phase do not want to describe their feelings at this point in the debriefing. An officer may say, "I felt just like he did" (indicating a neighbor who has just spoken). At that point, the facilitator may need to encourage the individual to speak by asking: What was the worst part of the experience for you? It is also possible for the reverse to occur. An officer may do little or no speaking during the fact phase and simply agree that the facts presented by his or her neighbors are correct. Yet, during the reaction phase, that same officer may voice emotions that are quite different from his or her neighbors.

In Mitchell's system, as in Bohl´s, the fourth phase is a feelings or reaction phase, during which the facilitator encourages participants to ventilate emotions. The major difference between the two approaches, however, is that Bohl tries to get at feelings by using information the participant already has provided. In contrast, Mitchell tries to get at feelings by asking: What was the worst thing about the event?

Phase 5. In Bohl′s model, phase 5, the **symptom phase**, is one in which participants describe what they experienced at the time and are still experiencing. Most of the symptoms that participants talk about are immediate physiological responses like nausea and time slowing down. The facilitator tries to validate the participants' experiences. For example, if someone says, "I felt sick to my stomach," then the facilitator validates by saying that anyone would feel sick in that situation. However, it is important for others in the group to validate as well. The officer needs to know that her or his coworkers had the same or similar reactions.

Phase 6. The **unfinished business** phase is one in which participants are asked: What in the present situation reminds you of a past experience? Do you want to talk about these other situations? There is no comparable phase in Mitchell's model. Dr. Bohl added the unfinished business phase because her experience showed that the incident for which the current debriefing was being conducted often acted as a catalyst to bring up reminders of prior events.

Phase 7. Phase 7 of Bohl´s model is an **educational or teaching** phase. Participants are told about how to deal with their families and their children. For police, a special problem is the fact that a child may have heard that the officer killed someone. Another possibility is that family members may experience vicarious symptoms. Therefore, it is important to educate participants not only about what they have experienced so far but also about what they may experience after the debriefing. For example, participants are told: You may not be able to sleep well tonight. You may find yourself arguing with your spouse a lot during the next few days. As in the symptoms phase, participants are reassured that their symptoms are normal and will go away. Feedback from police officers who have been debriefed makes it plain that they appreciate this attempt to prepare them, in a practical way, for the immediate future.

Phase 8. The **wrap-up** is a time when questions are answered and participants are asked about whether there is any information they want passed on to their supervisors.

Phase 9. The **round robin**. Each person is instructed to say anything that he or she wants to say. The remark can be addressed to anyone, but because others cannot respond directly, participants have a feeling of safety. The facilitator also contributes something at this time. The round robin phase constitutes an emotional ending. However, it is important to note that the emotions expressed in this phase are to be positive. For example, one police officer may say to another one, "I want you to know that I am glad you are my partner" or "I want you to know that Michael (a dead officer) loved you." Thus, the debriefing ends on an upbeat note, with hugs, handshakes and a show of relief. Participants seem to experience a strong sense of bonding.

In Dr. Bohl's debriefings, typically, participants do not leave but stay to talk informally with the facilitator, other members of the debriefing team, and each other. Before they leave, they receive handouts describing the initial symptoms experienced, symptoms they may experience later, ways to cope (e.g., exercise, meditation, talking to family members), and unsuccessful coping mechanisms to avoid (e.g., reliance on alcohol and drugs).

The Justification of Counseling in the Workplace

The following section is a very important topic for the Community Service Chaplain. Much of the chaplain's responsibility in the workplace environment will be interaction, counsel and guidance with employees and staff. This type of interaction must take on a different complexion than that of pastoral counseling. The dynamics of counseling in the workplace are vastly different from that of the pastor in a church environment. The consequences are greatly different for both the chaplain and the person the chaplain is guiding.

Counseling, or guidance in the work place must be seen very much in the context of the agency or workplace where the Community Service Chaplain does ministry. The response to this topic will be based on the policies and guidelines of the agency for which the chaplain works. Additionally, there will be unwritten policies or rather subjective interpretation by supervisors and staff as to when, if ever, counseling should be done in the workplace.

Chaplains will need to consider several items when addressing this issue. Among the items to consider will be the urgency of the need, the general acceptance of the chaplain on the site, the relationship of the counselee to the other employees in the agency, the appearance of propriety, the length of time needed to do the counseling and if the reason for counseling is job related. There will certainly be other considerations but these will offer the chaplain a general idea and direction to pursue when considering giving counsel in the workplace.

Urgency of the Need - The chaplain needs to determine if immediate intervention is needed or if the counseling session or debriefing can be postponed until after work hours. Example, if an employee has a panic or anxiety attack while in the workplace it will be essential to give immediate assistance. If an employee engages in fits of rage, anger or otherwise acts out of frustration, then the counseling would be most appropriate. The chaplain will always keep in mind that his/her counsel must always remain within the scope of the chaplain's training and skills.

The General Acceptance of the Chaplain on the Work Site. - This is a very important consideration. Even though the chaplain may be a volunteer with the agency, if the chaplain is not perceived as part of the staff, the counselee will not feel altogether comfortable in engaging in a counseling session during duty hours no matter how brief the session. Additionally, if the chaplain is not completely accepted as part of the agency... the other employees will see him or her as a distraction and deterrent to the mission as opposed to an asset.

The Relationship of the Counselee to other Employees. - This is an issue of which the chaplain must keep abreast. If the chaplain engages in "on site" counseling with an employee who is considered by his peers to be "non productive," then the chaplain will be seen as a contributor to such behavior. The need for the counseling may be genuine, but a disingenuous employee who uses the time of the chaplain for something, which could wait until after hours, may stymie the overall effectiveness of the chaplain and his/her ministry. The Community Service Chaplain must always be alert to this.

The Appearance of Propriety. - The Chaplain must be alert at all times to situations in which he/she presents themselves for service. While you have a much-needed ministry and service, and the motives of the chaplain are noble and Godly, counseling in the workplace must always be seen from a very proper, professional and Godly point of view. If the chaplain spends too much time behind closed doors with an employee of the opposite sex, the rumors will soon begin to run rampant. There will certainly be times that privacy and confidentiality are of the utmost importance, but where possible the chaplain shall put him/herself in a position to have both privacy and visibility at the same time.

Length of Time Needed to Counsel on the Job - When using agency time to address counseling needs of the employees, it is important to remember that the agency or firm is paying the employee while they are with you in a counseling session. Hence, the conscientious chaplain determines the amount of time necessary to address a specific need while on the job. The chaplain would best be advised to defuse an alarming situation as quickly as possible and then encourage the employee to meet after hours, during lunch, or at a mutually agreed upon time when the constraints of employment are not pressing.

Is the Counseling Job-Related? - Most employers will not mind the interruption of duty if they are aware that the employee being counseled by the chaplain on the job has a work-related difficulty or problem. Even if the problem is a "difference of opinion" with the administration, the employers will normally see on the job counseling as a way to appease both the employee and to be able to assist the employee with an immediate problem they are facing. The chaplain must help the employee and employer exercise integrity and honesty in these situations.

The Do's and Don'ts of Counseling in the Work Place.

While many of the Dos and Don'ts can be covered in the examples above, it is necessary to address a few other important items. When the Community Service Chaplain begins counseling in the workplace, he or she will begin a learning process that will be at the same time both pleasant and painful. The chaplain will slowly be brought into the confidence of the employees and employers regarding very intimate and personally important issues. Provided below are some Do's and Don'ts, that if followed, will save the chaplain much grief and frustration and will enhance his/her ability to continue to serve the agency to which God has called him/her.

Do .....

1. Speak positively at all times about the agency and its administration.

2. Treat all employees with similar respect.

3. Speak positively of fellow employees

4. Maintain complete confidentiality with the employees, even with items that to you may seem insignificant.

5. Take special note and recognize those who have received awards or honor for service to the agency.

6. Set regular "office hours" where possible. It will demonstrate discipline and accessibility.

7. Invest your time, talents and resources into the agency. It really will pay off.

8. Participate in the training and other "mandatory" requirements of the staff.

9. Utilize the Employee Assistance Office of the agency.

Don't ......

1. Fail to return calls made to you by employees.

2. Polarize only to the administration.

3. Violate a confidence.

4. Avoid insignificant jobs or jobs that others may not wish to do. You will get a reputation.

5. Get trapped into an employee grievance procedure.

6. Fail to refer to other agencies, too many pastors make this mistake, the chaplain should not

7. Speak ill of the Employee Assistance Officer

8. Compromise to become "one of the guys"... it does not pay dividends.

The Do's and Don'ts of counsel and guidance in the workplace can certainly be extrapolated depending on the type of agency, department or ministry.

Conclusion

Community Service Chaplaincy is definitely a ministry, which can change the dynamics of an agency, community and church. The Pastors and leaders of our ecclesiastical communities are charged with reaching the communities and the world on behalf of the Lord and Savior Jesus Christ. It is, in fact, a biblical command. This book allows us some tools that have been proven to work and be successful in allowing our churches and faith communities to reach into our communities.

It is the author's deepest concern and prayer that the tools you have received from this book will be implemented for Kingdom growth in your faith communities.

Table 1

<u>THE SYSTEMS OF THE BODY WHICH ARE
AFFECTED BY STRESS</u>

Specific Areas

Emotional

- Anxiety
- Panic
- Fear
- Depression
- Feeling overwhelmed

Behavioral

- Withdrawn
- Inability to rest
- Alcohol consumption
- Suspiciousness
- Antisocial acts

Physical

- Fatigue
- Chest pain
- Dizziness
- Elevated blood pressure
- Vomiting

Cognitive

- Confusion
- Loss of time
- disturbed thinking
- Nightmares

\-   Intrusive images

Table 2

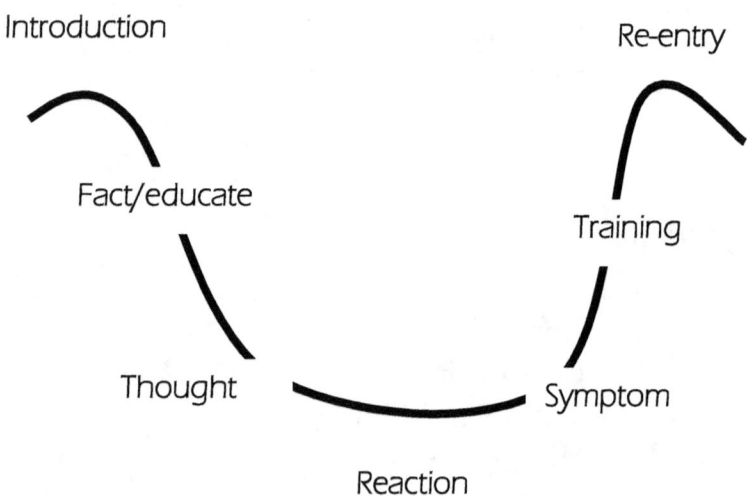

Introduction

Re-entry

Fact/educate

Training

Thought

Symptom

Reaction

Bibliography

Bull, Chris. "The Price of Honesty." The Advocate, 5 December 2000, 29. Database on-line. Available from Questia, http://www.questia.com/. Internet. Accessed 14 July 2005.

Bullis, Ronald K., and Cynthia S. Mazur. Legal Issues and Religious Counseling. 1st ed. Louisville, KY: Westminster John Knox Press, 1993.

Cleary, William, ed. Selving: Linking Work to Spirituality. Milwaukee, WI: Marquette University Press, 2000.

Cook, Alicia Skinner, and Daniel S. Dworkin. Helping the Bereaved: Therapeutic Interventions for Children, Adolescents, and Adults. New York: Basic Books, 1992.

Drakeman, Donald L. Church-State Constitutional Issues: Making Sense of the Establishment Clause. New York: Greenwood Press, 1991.

Finlay, Barbara. "Do Men and Women Have Different Goals for Ministry? Evidence from Seminarians." Sociology of Religion 57, no. 3 (1996): 311-318.

Hall, Douglas John. "Confessing Christ in a Post-Christendom Context." The Ecumenical Review 52, no. 3 (2000): 410. Database on-line.

Available from Questia, http://www.questia.com/. Internet. Accessed 14 July 2005.

Jacob, Walter and Moshe Zemer, eds. Crime and Punishment in Jewish Law: Essays and Responsa. New York: Berghahn Books, 1999.

Kurke, Martin I. and Ellen M. Scrivner, eds. Police Psychology into the 21st Century. Hillsdale, NJ: Lawrence Erlbaum Associates, 1995.

Lehman, Edward C. "Placement of Men and Women in the Ministry1." Review of Religious Research 22, no. 1 (1980): 18-40.

Lester, David, and Antoon A. Leenaars. "Gun Control and Rates of Firearms Violence in Canada and the United States: A Comment." Canadian Journal of Criminology 36, no. 4 (1994): 462-463. Database on-line. Available from Questia, http://www.questia.com/. Internet. Accessed 14 July 2005.

Lull, Timothy F. "Reshaping the Mission of the CHURCH." USA Today (Society for the Advancement of Education), July 2000, 58. Database on-line. Available from Questia, http://www.questia.com/. Internet. Accessed 14 July 2005.

Masin, Sandra. "Shakopee Volunteers Help Inmates and Offenders in the Community." Corrections Today, August 1993, 128+. Database on-line. Available from Questia, http://www.questia.com/. Internet. Accessed 14 July 2005.

Steffenhagen, R. A., and Jeff D. Burns. The Social Dynamics of Self-Esteem: Theory to Therapy. New York: Praeger, 1987.

Thiemann, Ronald F. A Dilemma for Democracy A Dilemma for Democracy. Washington, DC: Georgetown University Press, 1996.

Thomas, L. Eugene and Susan A. Eisenhandler, eds. Aging and the Religious Dimension. Westport, CT: Auburn House, 1994.

Viteritti, Joseph P. "Davey's Plea: Blaine, Blair, Witters, and the Protection of Religious Freedom." Harvard Journal of Law & Public Policy

27, no. 1 (2003): 299+. Database on-line. Available from Questia, http://www.questia.com/. Internet. Accessed 14 July 2005.

Wright, Stephen G, and Jean Sayre-Adams. Sacred Space: Right Relationship and Spirituality in Healthcare. Edinburgh: Churchill Livingstone, 2000.

Research Services, The Lutheran Church, Missouri Synod: Clergy Who Leave the Parish Ministry and Why. A Quarterly Review of Religious Research, Vol 2, Number 2, March 2004

Hartung, Bruce M. The Health of the Workers of the Church, (Part one).

Krakower, Karen. Clergy in Crisis: Who Ministers to the Minister? Mosaic Publication, 1997.